CRASH COURSE IN

ARCHITECTURE

CRASH COURSE IN
ARCHITECTURE

EVA HOWARTH

ERIC DOBBY PUBLISHING

This edition published 1994 by
Eric Dobby Publishing Ltd

British Library Cataloguing in Publication Data
Crash course in architecture.
  I. Western visual arts, history
  I. Howarth, Eva
  709

ISBN 1-85882-035-9

Designed by Tim Scott
Typeset by Spectrum Typesetting Ltd, London
Origination by Columbia Offset Ltd
Printed and bound in Italy

ERIC DOBBY PUBLISHING LTD
12 WARNFORD ROAD
ORPINGTON
KENT BR6 6LW

FRONTISPIECE *Mainz Cathedral (west facade)*

The author would like to acknowledge the assistance received from David Brady, James Gibbs and Maurice Hughes, who acted as consultants. Peter Hailly, together with James Gibbs and Morris Hughes, provided illustrations for the text.

Contents

INTRODUCTION

Byzantine and Baroque, architrave and apse. Such words pepper the guidebooks and roll off the tourist guides' tongues.

Of course we know what they mean more or less, and yet the thousands, or hundreds of thousands, of people who enjoy visiting castles and cathedrals, palaces and piazzas would often like to know rather more about what they are seeing.

They do not seek to become experts, but it would give them pleasure to know just why a building belongs to a particular style and to be able to state with confidence the century or centuries in which it was built. This book has been written for all such people.

You can take it with you wherever you go. So, standing in the cathedral nave or looking at the façade of a stately home, you can consult it and find immediately the answers to the questions which have been puzzling you – why a building is a fine example of a particular style, for example, and even when it was constructed.

The illustrated guide to architectural features on page 150 is particularly helpful. Let us suppose you are in a church. You can see the shapes of the windows and the doors. By looking at the guide to architectural features you can find similar windows and doors illustrated, and in this way you are able to identify them as, say, Romanesque. You then turn to the chapter on Romanesque architecture in the book.

In addition to information on the architecture of the past, this book also includes an important section about the architecture of the present.

Do not be misled by the simplicity of what you read here. There is true expertise behind every chapter, but it is all presented in such a way that you can consult it wherever you are and remember it easily.

Salisbury Cathedral tower

Chronology

CLASSICAL GREECE

To understand and enjoy the architecture of classical Greece we must approach it in the manner of the archaeologist. In other words, what we see is only part of the picture. The rest must be filled in by imagination based on study. This can be a rewarding exercise, not least because of the quality of Greek achievement.

Among the various city-states in Greece, Athens was artistically pre-eminent. It was a small town with some 50,000 freemen, yet it controlled an empire.

In the fifth century BC architecture, sculpture and drama in Athens reached levels not far short of perfection. Indeed, if asked to name the most perfect building in the world, many people would choose the Parthenon, which was built in the fifth century as the chief temple of Athena on the Acropolis.

Yet the Parthenon we see today is largely a ruin. Originally it contained a gold and ivory statue of Athena, but this was subsequently taken away. In the sixth century AD the temple was turned into a church, and the inner columns and roof were removed. Later it became a mosque and, in the seventeenth century, an ammunition store. After that the

The Parthenon

The column shaft rose from the base and was topped by the capital, upon which rested at least three layers of entablature: the architrave (lower), frieze (middle) and cornice (upper).

damage was more gradual.

Even so, in comparison with the other buildings of the extraordinary civilization which once flourished in Greece, the Parthenon is well preserved. That is the measure of our loss and also of the challenge to those who go today to look at what remains.

What makes even the ruin of the Parthenon so memorable? Principally purity of style, perfect harmony and technical perfection.

HOW TO RECOGNIZE A CLASSICAL GREEK BUILDING

The so-called "post-and-lintel" type of construction is the term used to describe standard Greek practice. Greek buildings were composed entirely of horizontal blocks supported by columns and walls. Straight lines predominated and, in marked contrast with all later styles, there were no arches or curves.

The two main components of a building are the **entablature** and the **column.** Within the entablature are the **cornice,** the **frieze,** and the **architrave.** The column is made up of the **capital,** the **shaft,** and the **base.**

TEMPLES

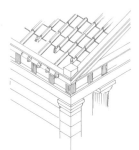

Temple roof corner

To the Greeks, the most important buildings were temples. Some temples were circular in shape, but the majority were rectangular. A temple was always built on an elevated platform with steps leading up to it. These steps were too high for human legs, and at one point normal-sized steps were cut into them.

The main entrance always faced east. In front of the temple was an open **portico** supported by columns with a corresponding portico at the opposite end of the building.

The columns of the portico continued along the two sides of the temple and joined the columns of the portico at the back. In this way

Temple portico

Relief carving (water spout)

symmetry was achieved irrespective of the direction from which the building was seen.

The low, slanting roof was constructed from wooden rafters and covered with thin marble or terracotta tiles. Shallow **pediments** surmounted the whole length of both the east and west façades. There were very few windows. Light came in mainly through the doorway and skylights.

Christian churches are built to house the congregation who come to worship. A Greek temple was considered the private abode of a deity, and only the priests were allowed to enter. The altar was always on the outside of the building, either on top or in front of the main steps, and all the rituals and festivities were held outside.

A temple was decorated in the brightest of colours. There were statues in the front of the building and beautiful relief carvings, especially on the pediments and **friezes.**

The temple consisted usually of two chambers. The smaller chamber at the back, the treasury, was used mainly to store the offerings made to the deity. The larger chamber (the naos) housed the statue of the god or goddess to whom the temple was dedicated.

When the huge ceremonial double doors were open, the rays of the morning sun would fall directly on to the statue of the deity. This must have been an impressive sight, for the statues were often colossal – some were more than 12 metres (13 yards) high – and covered

The temple contained two inner chambers: one small, in the rear (the treasury); and a larger chamber (the naos), which contained a statue of the god to whom the temple was dedicated.

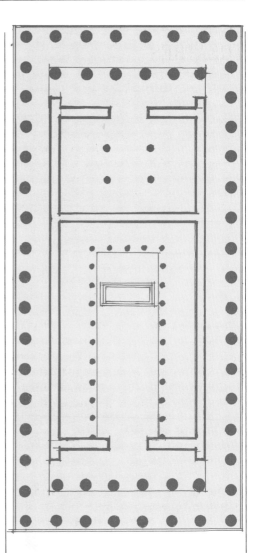

Ceremonial door

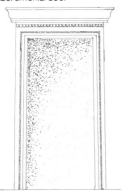

in ivory, gold and semi-precious stones. They were also painted by artists whose task it was to enrich the statue even further.

Regular festivals were held, when the whole of the populace walked in procession to the temple, bringing the sacrificial animals. After the priests had ritually killed the animals they sprinkled them with scent and burnt them on the temple fires. It was believed that the deity would smell the scent and thereby know that the people had gathered there and held a festival in his or her honour.

In Athens the statue of the goddess of the city, Athene, even received a new dress at each annual festival.

THEATRES

Next in importance to the temples were the Greek theatres. Open-air theatres were usually cut into the side of a hill. Some seated as many as 30,000, yet both vision and acoustics were excellent. It was in these huge open-air theatres that the works of Aeschylus, Sophocles, Euripides and Aristophanes were performed.

The central part of the theatre was reserved for the chorus, an indispensable part of Greek drama. The auditorium formed a semi-circle around it. The front rows, with beautifully carved marble seats, were reserved for the priests and important dignitaries. Behind the chorus was a long, narrow stage with a building which served both as a store room and a changing room.

Many of the plays were concerned with major public and religious issues, and attendance at the theatre was not only a pleasure but also a civic duty for all freemen of Athens.

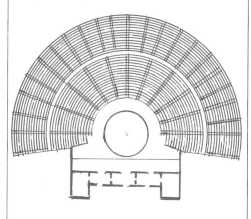

Greek theatre

GREEK ORDERS

There are three different types or styles of order (column) in Greek architecture: Doric, Ionic and Corinthian.

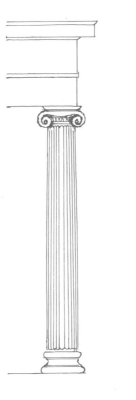

Greek Orders: Doric (left),
Ionic (middle) and Corinthian
(right).

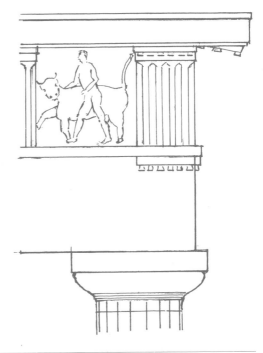

Doric capital

Ionic capital

Corinthian capital

The relative proportions of base, shaft and capital varied in the different types of order. The Romans adapted the Greek orders for their own purposes, but in general Roman orders were lighter, and more heavily decorated.

17

Doric

The Doric order is the most massive of the three. It is the only style in which the column has no base and the shaft is placed directly on the platform. The shaft itself is grooved and the grooves meet in a sharp edge. The capital can be described as a **plain convex moulding.**

The architrave can be plain or decorated with intermittent rows of small triangular carvings. The frieze is decorated with a series of tablets with vertical flutings, alternating with square spaces which were either left plain or decorated with relief carvings.

Ionic

In the Ionic order the shaft is taller and more slender. The grooves on the shaft are separated by flat bands.

Occasionally the shafts are replaced by female figures (caryatids). According to legend, they represent the women from an ancient tribe whom the Greeks captured and enslaved.

Caryatid

The capital has two sets of spirals, rather like a roll of paper with its ends curled towards each other.

The architrave is made up of three horizontal planes, each projecting slightly beyond the one below. The frieze can be plain or sculptured. The cornice in the Ionic order is often decorated with rows of small blocks which look like teeth and are called **dentals.**

Corinthian

The Corinthian order is similar to the Ionic. The main difference is in the capital, which is much more richly decorated.

A Corinthian capital is like an inverted bell. Some of them are decorated with acanthus leaves surmounted by four symmetrical scrolls. In others lotus or palm leaves replace the scrolls.

Acanthus scroll

MATHEMATICAL RULES IN GREEK ARCHITECTURE

The Greeks never used more than one style for the whole of a building. The only exception to this rule was to have one order for the exterior and another for the interior. As a result it is relatively easy to decide the style of any Greek building, even one in ruins, by looking at a capital, a segment of a column or part of an entablature.

All the measurements used by the architects, such as the height of a column, were expressed in multiples of the diameter at the base of the shaft.

Each order had its own rules concerning the size of its component parts. For example, the height of a Doric column is between four and six times the diameter of its base. The height of an Ionic column is nine times, and the height of a Corinthian column ten times the diameter of its base. Similar rules governed even the smallest component of a building.

The system had many advantages. One was that while only a man of great talent could build a masterpiece, even a mediocre architect, working within the rules, could produce a passable result.

IN SEARCH OF PERFECTION

One of the great strengths of Greek architects was their skill in creating the appearance of perfect symmetry. They achieved this partly by eliminating the optical illusions to which all buildings are to some extent subject, a technique known as **entasis.**

Seen from a certain distance all straight lines, vertical or horizontal, seem slightly concave at the middle. To counteract this Greek architects made the lines of the buildings correspondingly convex.

In the same way distances between columns seem to vary when in fact they are mathematically exactly equal. Greek architects therefore varied the spacing of their columns.

These are only two out of a number of techniques used to correct optical illusions and achieve buildings approaching perfection.

Greek temple

The adjustments were small and delicate. For example, the horizontal line of an entablature of over 60 metres (200 ft) needed to curve upwards only 10 cm (5in) at its centre for the concave appearance to be eliminated. The techniques required to make these adjustments were time-consuming and very expensive, and they were used only for the most important buildings, such as temples.

Although little of ancient Greek architecture remains in its original form, its influence has been enormous. The ancient Greeks took their styles to the lands which they colonized – for example Sicily and much of the Mediterranean littoral – and when Greece itself became a Roman colony in the second century BC the Romans happily adopted the styles of what they instinctively recognized as fine art.

Greek influence has inspired a number of classical revivals and it continues to be evident in architecture even today.

Greek decoration (vase, detail)

Chronology

IMPERIAL ROME

**1st Century BC–
4th Century AD**

Most of the Greek city-states were no bigger than what we now call small towns or large villages. Rome, by contrast, was a city with perhaps a million inhabitants. For architects and town planners this meant that new problems required new solutions. Continuous supplies of food and water brought in from outside, housing on a huge scale, markets and mass entertainments were only a few of the needs which engineers and builders now had to meet.

Rome was an imperial capital, which Augustus, the first Emperor, was determined to make worthy of the position it held in the known world. In his own words: 'I found Rome a city of brick and left it a city of marble'. As a consequence of all this the variety of buildings which Rome required was quite unprecedented.

The great age of ancient Roman architecture coincided roughly with the period of the empire and lasted some four hundred years

Roman architecture incorporated Greek features on a larger scale

from the accession of Augustus in 27 BC.

Although relatively little of what was built in those four centuries remains intact, we are still able to picture Roman cities as they once were, largely through the skill of archaeologists, and partly because of some strange accidents.

One such accident was the eruption of Vesuvius in AD 79, which buried the town of

Roman rounded arches

Pompeii in lava and thereby preserved it. As a result we can see today the regular pattern of the streets. We know where the theatres and temples, fountains and shrines, baths and meat market were, and what they looked like. We can see at a glance how many rooms there were in private houses and how big the shops were. We can even tell from inscriptions that Pompeii had a mixed population, including Greeks and Jews.

As the Roman empire expanded, cities built in the Roman style came into being in various parts of Europe, North Africa and Asia Minor. The legions were expected to stay in occupation for long periods. Local governors were men of consequence who expected to live well. So the forums and baths, theatres and temples which characterized Roman cities sprang up beyond the Alps and the Rhine and the English Channel.

Some of these cities are still being excavated and continue to add to our knowledge of Roman architecture.

HOW TO RECOGNIZE A ROMAN BUILDING

The rounded arch and the classical orders were predominant features. Among the great variety of Roman buildings were **temples, basilicas, triumphal arches, theatres, baths, bridges, aqueducts** and **villas.**

GREEK INFLUENCE

Greek influence on Roman architecture was profound, particularly after Greece became a Roman province in the second century BC. Many of Rome's outstanding buildings were indeed built by Greeks.

Greek architecture was based on horizontal and vertical components only. This imposed certain technical limitations. For example, the

Greek-based horizontal and vertical construction

maximum span possible between columns was 5 to 6 metres (16 to 19½ ft), and buildings

Combined column and rounded arch

could be no more than two storeys high. The limiting factor was the weight that a column could support.

Given the relatively small scale of Greek buildings, these limitations were of little importance. The Romans, by contrast, wanted taller buildings constructed on a much more lavish scale. They succeeded largely through an ingenious combination of the column with the **rounded arch,** a system which gives a very much higher load-bearing capacity.

Smaller buildings or buildings of no more than one storey high, such as temples, continued to be built in the Greek style. For larger buildings, or for buildings of more than one storey, the Romans made use of the rounded arch. The Greek orders served mainly as decoration in such buildings.

ROMAN ORDERS

The Romans had five different styles or orders. Three were borrowed directly from the Greeks: Doric – the plainest and sturdiest; Ionic – with fluted capitals; and Corinthian – in which the capital is decorated with acanthus leaves. This last order was the most popular among the Romans.

Greek orders used by the Romans: Doric (left), Ionic (middle) and Corinthian (right).

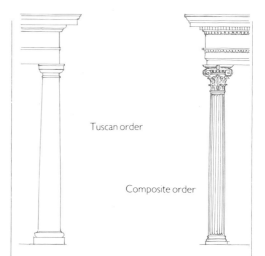

Tuscan order

Composite order

The two styles which the Romans added were Tuscan – an even simpler form of Doric; and Composite – a richer form of Corinthian.

In Roman buildings of more than one storey the orders were placed one above the other and usually in a prescribed sequence. The lowest would be the Doric, above it the Ionic, and above that the Corinthian.

Doors and windows were rectangular and were usually framed by different styles of moulding. In the doors the opening was reduced to human proportions. The space at both sides of the opening was usually filled in by columns. In many of the doors the space above the opening was filled in by an ornate bronze grille.

Building materials were brick, tiles, cement, concrete and iron. The Romans developed concrete, an extremely hard and durable material, in the second century BC. Concrete was also easier to handle and more economical than other materials, and it soon came into common use. To make it more attractive in appearance, concrete was faced with stone, plaster, stucco or marble.

Concrete made possible the construction of the great Roman **vaults** and **domes**. The spans of many vaults – some over 50 metres (55 yards) in diameter – were not equalled until the development of steel construction in the 19th century.

Roman domes are sometimes described as

Doorway with columns and grille

'saucer domes' because of their shape. In comparison with domes of later periods they are comparatively shallow.

TEMPLES

More than any other type of Roman building the temples, especially the early ones, strongly resembled their Greek prototypes. Many of the Roman temples survived because at later dates they were converted into Christian churches.

Temples were built on high podiums with a flight of steps leading up to the building. Rectangular temples had a deep portico in the front, with the columns continuing along the two sides of the building. Along the sides the columns either formed a **colonnade** or were attached to the walls. In round temples the

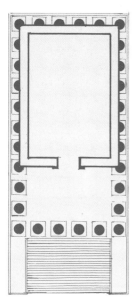

Roman temple (ground-plan)

Round temple

Elaborate Corinthian orders
and colonnade

colonnade went all around the building.

The roofs were low-pitched with correspondingly shallow pediments. The name of the deity to whom the temple was dedicated was usually cut into the stone below the pediment.

Most Roman temples were built in the elaborate Corinthian or Ionic orders. The severe Doric order was very rarely used.

The altar was always on the outside of the building, and the ceremonies took place in the open.

The interiors of the early temples tended to be very plain. This changed dramatically in imperial times, when some of the interiors created were truly magnificent.

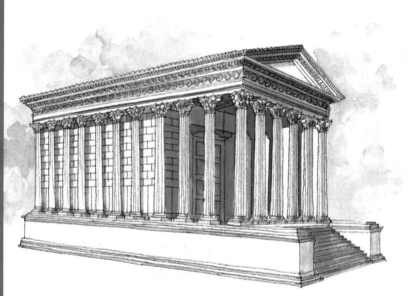

The Pantheon, Rome (interior)

BASILICAS

The Roman basilica was both a hall of justice and a place for business transactions.

The ground-plan of the building was rectangular. On the inside it was divided by two rows of columns into a central nave and two aisles.

The basilica had a simple trussed timber roof

Basilica (interior)

31

or a vaulted structure, which was either a **barrel vault** or a **groined vault.** Domes were a common feature. Light was let in through windows above the aisles.

One end of the building – or in some cases both ends – terminated in an **apse,** where the sacrificial altar was to be found. At ceremonies or after important decisions had been taken it was usual for sacrifices to be offered at the altar.

Public bath

PUBLIC BATHS

At one time in Imperial Rome alone there were over 800 public baths of different sizes and standards. The largest and most luxurious baths were centres of social life. They had heated halls for the winter and shaded gardens for the summer. Here philosophers exchanged ideas, authors read from their latest works, and the news of the day was discussed. Some of the buildings also housed theatres, sports stadia and restaurants. The largest public baths could accommodate over 3000 people at a time.

The baths themselves consisted of a series of hot and cold rooms. The last to be visited was usually an open-air swimming pool. They were heated in the same way as private houses. Hot air from furnaces in the basement passed through hollow tiles and bricks in the walls and floors. The temperature in the different rooms could be regulated exactly to meet requirements.

The whole of each building was richly decorated. Marble and mosaic covered the walls and floors. Wall niches held statuary. Bronze was commonly used for door and window screens. Marble columns supported gilded capitals. Service was provided by means of underground passage-ways, through which slaves could move swiftly and without disturbing anyone.

THEATRES

The main components of the theatres were the semi-circular **auditorium,** the **orchestra** and the **stage**. The stage stretched from one side of the semi-circle to the other. Behind the stage the so-called 'stage-building', often two or three storeys high and elaborately decorated, was used mainly as the actors'

Roman theatre

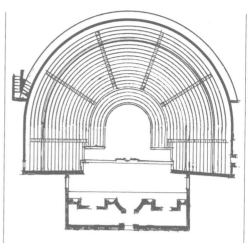

dressing-room.

If an actor entered from the centre door it indicated that the character he was playing had come from the palace. Entrance from one side door meant that he had come from the city or the forum, and from the other that he had come from the country.

AMPHITHEATRES

These were used mainly for gladiatorial combats and similar spectacles, which usually ended in the killing of the vanquished.

The central **arena** was entirely surrounded by tiered seating. Underneath the arena were

Amphitheatre

rooms for the gladiators and other unfortunate human participants, and cages for the animals.

The best seats were reserved for state officials. Above them were those for the rich or the nobles, and higher still the seats for the rest of the populace. Seats were numbered and presumably, therefore, could be reserved.

Sophisticated stage techniques made spectacular displays possible. The whole of the arena, for example, could be flooded and a mock naval battle staged.

The Coliseum

TRIUMPHAL ARCHES

Triumphal arches commemorated great military victories and other important events. They were often situated astride a main road leading into a city and were composed either of one or of three arches.

There was usually a column on each side of the arch and Corinthian or Composite orders were most commonly used. Elaborate carvings decorated the space below the columns and around and underneath the arches and friezes.

Triumphal arch

The part above the entablature was called the **attic.** This contained the dedicatory inscription. Above the attic there was usually a large sculptured group, often in the form of figures driving a chariot with four or six horses.

AQUEDUCTS AND BRIDGES

Aqueduct

The Romans raised engineering to the level of art. By doing so they made utilitarian buildings, such as bridges and aqueducts, both majestic and beautiful.

Aqueducts were built from arches in one, two or three tiers. The water was carried in a cement-lined channel which ran along the top.

Some aqueducts were many kilometres in length and towered over the countryside. It was estimated that at one time 1500 million litres (330 million gallons) of water a day from 11 great aqueducts were pouring into Rome. From the aqueducts the water was diverted into pipes and distributed throughout the city. The rich often had their own water supply, while the rest of the population had to rely on communal wells.

Roman bridges were simple but extremely solid structures. Some indeed are still in use and able to carry heavy traffic today.

DOMESTIC ARCHITECTURE

The principal forms of Roman domestic architecture were the town house (domus); the apartment house (insula); and the country house (villa).

Seen from the outside the houses of even the richest Romans were quite plain. Roman houses normally had no windows except when part of the ground floor was let off as a shop, as happened, for example, in Pompeii.

The interior of a house was planned around one or more courtyards. A passage led from the front door to a court known as an **atrium**. The atrium was covered except for an open section in the centre of the roof, which admitted light. It also let in rain, which was collected in a cistern or pool situated below the opening.

In many houses there was a second or inner court known as a peristyle. This was a colonnaded walk surrounding a garden with fountains or statues. The most luxurious villas had several courts.

The various rooms were grouped round the courts. In addition to dining room, reception

Shops occasionally flanked the street entrance (bottom), from which a passage led to a covered court (the atrium). Further back, an inner court (the peristyle), consisted of a colonnaded walk surrounding a garden.

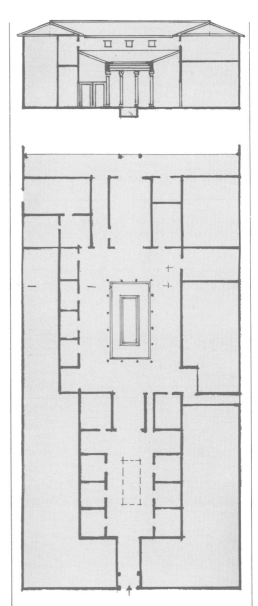

rooms, bedrooms and games rooms, these would include a room for the household gods.

The rooms in the houses of the well-to-do were evidence of a high, even luxurious standard of living and of advanced technology. The houses were comfortable as well as elegant and were well equipped with central heating and baths.

The living rooms and reception rooms were richly decorated. The floors were laid with

Roman house (interior)

mosaics or coloured marble. **Frescoes** covered the walls. In some houses wall surfaces were divided into panels of painted **stucco.**

Another practice was to paint the interior walls with outdoor scenes to create the impression that the walls had disappeared. Human figures were sometimes included in the paintings, usually in scenes from everyday life.

The main ornamental motifs were acanthus leaves and scrolls. Panels and borders were decorated with scrollwork and with representations of animals, plants and mythological figures. Birds, griffins, ivy and cupids were particularly popular.

Chronology

380	Christianity declared official religion in the Roman Empire
406	Vandals invade Gaul
410	Alaric the Goth sacks Rome
493	Emperor Theodoric establishes his residence in Ravenna
496	King Clovis of Merovingians baptized a Christian
565	Death of the Emperor Justinian
594	Gregory of Tours completes his *History of the Franks*
604	Death of Pope Gregory the Great
711	Muslim invasion of Spain
768	Death of King Pippin of the Franks
800	Charlemagne becomes Emperor
878	Muslims conquer Sicily
910	Abbey of Cluny founded

THE EARLY CHRISTIAN AND BYZANTINE PERIOD

3rd – 11th Century

The two principal architectural styles that developed between the middle years of the Roman Empire and the first millennium AD are known as Early Christian and Byzantine.

THE EARLY CHRISTIAN PERIOD

Basilica (interior)

So long as they were a prohibited sect Christians had to meet in secret, in private houses and in the catacombs. But in 313 the Emperor Constantine issued the Edict of Milan, which gave Christians the right to practise their religion openly. Twelve years later the Emperor himself was converted and in 380 Christianity became an official religion of the Roman Empire. Consequently, Christian church architecture does not begin until some three centuries after the Crucifixion.

HOW TO RECOGNIZE AN EARLY CHRISTIAN CHURCH

Early Christian churches are characterized by rectangular ground-plans. It was the basilica, rather than the temple, which became the common architectural prototype of the Early Christian church. The structure was spacious enough to hold a large congregation. The nave was uninterrupted by columns and gave a clear field of vision to the worshippers. The buildings were comparatively inexpensive to put up, which to the early Christians was an important consideration. They were usually about twice as long as they were wide and the entrance was always from the west.

The exterior was rather severe and relieved only by a front portico which extended across the whole width of the building. Those who were not allowed to enter the church because of their sins could stand in the portico and listen to the service from there.

The eastern end of the building took the form of a semi-circle – called an **apse** – with the altar in front of it. The rest of the interior was divided by two rows of arcades into a **nave** and two or more **aisles.** The walls above the arcades were flat, allowing spaces for frescoes or mosaics. Above these were the windows, which were surrounded by rounded arches. The **coffered** or **hammer-beam** roofs were made of wood, with either one or two supporting posts.

Basilica (ground-plan)

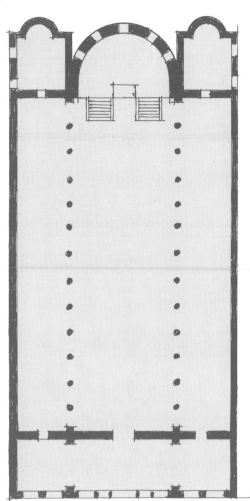

The early **baptisteries** were separate buildings and were circular or polygonal in shape. Light came in from a central dome. Only from the fifth century onward were baptisteries placed beside churches or attached to them.

The **font** was always in the centre of the baptistery and was usually a small-scale copy of the building itself. The fonts may seem surprisingly large. The reason for this is that in the early Christian period adults had to be fully immersed when baptized.

· The very high bell-tower next to the church served not only as an important landmark but also as a watchtower against possible attacks.

Byzantine church

THE EASTERN EMPIRE

After the division of the Empire into its eastern and western parts, and the subsequent collapse of the power of Rome, the Byzantine Empire continued to flourish. It developed its own characteristic architectural style, in which eastern influence greatly modified classical tradition.

In the sixth century the Byzantine Emperor Justinian tried unsuccessfully to recapture the territory of the former Roman Empire. His Italian capital was for a time Ravenna, and it is there that some of the greatest Byzantine churches in western Europe are to be found.

HOW TO RECOGNIZE A BYZANTINE CHURCH

The brilliant **mosaics** in the interiors of Byzantine churches are their most recognizable feature. The ground-plan could be basilican, cruciform, circular or polygonal.

The main entrance was from the west and the altar was always at the eastern end of the church.

The principal building material was brick, arranged in decorative patterns or covered in plaster. Roofs were either tiled or covered by sheets of lead.

Byzantine church (interior)

From the outside the buildings look rather plain, with austere entrances flanked by blind arcades. The grilled windows are small and were filled in with thin sheets of marble or parchment.

In vivid contrast the interiors glow with the rich, jewel-like colours of the mosaics, which decorate the walls, domes and vaults. The predominant colours are blue and gold. There are few columns and pillars, and as a result there is an almost unrestricted view of the mosaics. The subjects depicted are either scenes from the Bible or the imperial court.

Mosaic is made up of small cubes of marble or glass set in cement. The cement was prepared in a number of layers. When the final layer was in place the design was frescoed on to the damp cement. The cubes were then placed in the cement following the outlines of the design.

Byzantine capital

Byzantine capital

The last layer of the cement was put on unevenly, so that when the cubes were set in, the faces of the different cubes were at an angle to each other and reflected light from one cube to another. From this comes the almost magical impression of light and depth which mosaics convey. Modern mosaics, by contrast, are normally put on evenly and so fail to create this effect.

Richly grained marble was used to cover other parts of the walls and around the base of the piers. The floors were covered with inlaid marble or mosaics.

Byzantine dome

Byzantine columns and capitals are easily distinguished from the classical prototypes. Many of the capitals are surmounted by a large block of stone, which provides a broad base for the arch above. It was common practice to carve the monogram of the emperor or another rich patron on the capital.

The carvings on the capitals were created by deeply incised lines and drilled holes, giving a strongly defined black and white effect. The most popular forms of capital were the basket and the cubical.

From a structural point of view the dome is the most important feature of a Byzantine church. Unlike the Roman domes, which were all placed over round openings, Byzantine architects developed a system of construction which enabled them to place a dome over a square opening. This major advance was to have important consequences in Renaissance architecture.

Human figures do not appear in Byzantine sculpture. (A prohibition to the same effect is of course to be found in the Judaic and Islamic traditions.) Decorative effects were achieved with scrolls, circles and other geometric forms or by depicting leaves and flowers. Wind-blown acanthus leaves were a popular subject.

Chronology

THE MOORISH STYLE IN WESTERN EUROPE

8th – 15th Century

After the death of Mohammed in 632, Islam spread with phenomenal speed. Within a hundred and twenty years its followers dominated an area which included Kashmir, Persia, the Arabian Peninsula, the whole of the North African coast and the greater part of Spain and Portugal.

Although the Moors were in Spain for well over seven hundred years, from 709 to 1492, lamentably little of their architecture has survived. What there is consists largely of religious buildings and fortifications.

Moorish arches

HOW TO RECOGNIZE A MOORISH BUILDING

The single most obvious feature of Moorish architecture is the **horseshoe-shaped arch.** After about the tenth century the arches, instead of being fully rounded, were usually slightly pointed at the top. This shape, in turn, developed into a number of decorative and imaginative forms, such as the **poly-lobed** arch, in which the outline is broken up into a number of smaller arches. It was also common practice for the entire arch to be framed in an elaborately carved rectangle.

Blind arches (filled-in arches placed against a wall) were often used alone or to form complex patterns on the façades of buildings. The commonest of these were the interlacing arches.

Sometimes arches were made up from different materials – for example, a mixture of red brick and white stone, which provided a brilliant colour contrast.

RELIGIOUS BUILDINGS

The mosque is normally a low, rectangular structure, rather plain-looking from the outside and built from baked brick or sculptured stone. Roofs were usually unobtrusive, with a very slight slope, and covered with glazed tiles.

The rather ordinary looking main doors were flanked by arches, which were frequently re-used Roman columns and capitals.

The interior consisted of an open courtyard and the main building. The courtyard would have a fountain or some other source of clear water, with orange and date trees providing shade. Muslims attach great importance to personal cleanliness, and it is laid down in the Koran that worshippers must wash their hands and feet before prayer. Shoes have to be

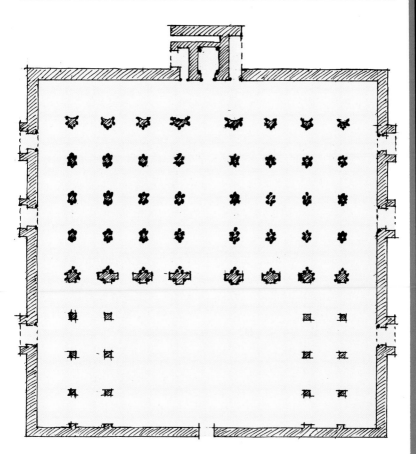

Mosque (ground-plan)

removed before entering the mosque from the courtyard.

Fountains and pools were features of Moorish domestic as well as religious architecture. Some Moorish mansions even had artificial lakes, and it was said that where a Greek would put up a statue, or a Christian a crucifix, an Arab would construct a fountain or dig a well.

The main building is divided into a series of naves formed by rows of slim columns supporting elaborate arches. There is a theory that the interior was intended to resemble a forest, symbolizing the Moors' original homeland in North Africa. All the naves are of equal height, indicating that all are equal in prayer.

The congregation kneels or sits on carpets placed on the floor. There is no seating.

The end wall, opposite the entrance, called the **Quibla** wall, always faces towards Mecca,

Moorish interior

the burial place of Mohammed. A semi-circular or polygonal niche in the Quibla wall is the holiest part of the mosque. It is called the **Mihrab** and as a rule is decorated with tiles bearing inscriptions from the Koran.

The Koran strictly forbade the portrayal of human and animal figures. Instead Islamic craftsmen developed the use of spiral and geometric shapes for decorative purposes. The term **'arabesque'** was coined in Europe during the Renaissance. It can be described as a continuously curving line which repeatedly divides to form secondary lines. This kind of decoration was frequently used on both the exterior and the interior of buildings.

Arabic calligraphy can also be very decorative on tiles or wall surfaces, and texts from the Koran were often inscribed in this way. Mosaics were another popular form of decoration.

Next to the mosque stood the **minaret,** a tall, slim, square-based tower, from which five times a day a crier called the faithful to prayer. Islamic artistic and architectural styles survived in Spain long after the Moorish occupation came to an end. Their influence on the design of Christian buildings has continued down to the present time.

Among the styles which developed through Islamic influence were the so-called **Mudejar,** which is part Islamic and part Gothic, and the **Mozarabic,** a blend of the Christian and the Arabic which became popular during the period of Moorish occupation. The word 'Mozarab' acquired more than one meaning. Significantly, at least as far as architecture was concerned, the Moors in Spain applied it to those who lived with and tried to imitate Arabs.

Such was the superiority of Islamic craftsmen that Arab builders, stonemasons, painters and mosaic workers were frequently employed by Christians to build churches as well as secular buildings.

Chronology

THE ROMANESQUE STYLE

11th – 12th Century

The word 'Romanesque' was coined in the 19th century to describe the architecture of the 11th and 12th centuries and means 'in the Roman style'.

In the dark ages which followed the collapse of the Roman Empire there was little architecture of distinction. Builders in the 11th century, looking for an ideal, turned to the architecture of ancient Rome. Yet, while adapting Roman methods and even pillaging Roman buildings to obtain their materials, the architects of the 11th century developed a distinct style of their own which was greatly inspired by Christianity.

Of the buildings which have survived from the Romanesque period a number are fortified castles. Most of the others are churches.

Romansque arcade

Romanesque church

HOW TO RECOGNIZE A ROMANESQUE CHURCH

The **rounded arch**, the most distinctive characteristic of Romanesque architecture can be seen in doors, windows, arcades, vaulted ceilings and in many decorative features.

The earliest churches had wooden roofs, which sooner or later burned down. They were particularly liable to catch fire because of the many candles and blazing torches which were used to light the churches.

Gradually in Romanesque churches the vaults came to be built of stone. The extra weight exerted great pressure on the rest of the building, and massive exterior walls were needed to support this weight. Shallow **buttresses** leaning against the walls served to give additional support.

Round, square or octagonal towers with their own steep roofs and of considerable height draw the eye upwards and relieve the heavy outline of the building. Two of the most prominent towers are those which flank the west door. Another is commonly found directly above the point where the nave crosses the **transept**. Pitched roofs with gables are another characteristic feature of Romanesque churches.

Pilasters connected by arched mouldings

Walls and towers are as a rule decorated with pilaster strips connected by arched mouldings, by real or blind arcades and by rows of windows. Dwarf arcades frequently encircle the towers just below the level of the roof.

Corbels, which are small projecting blocks of stone, often finely carved, are used as decoration or to support other decorative features such as sculptures. Carvings and sculptures are the principal forms of decoration on the main façade.

Doors are deeply set and the doorways flanked by a series of receding columns. Above the columns semi-circular arches recede in the same way. Above the door is a horizontal beam. The area between the beam and the arch above it, the tympanum, is usually filled with sculptures portraying biblical themes.

The depth of the doorways shows how extraordinarily thick these walls are, some more than six metres (20ft). An interesting feature of the door itself is the iron and bronze

Tympanum with biblical theme

Ironwork bracket

work. Many original locks, hinges and door-knockers can still be seen.

Windows were comparatively small and narrow. They were made to look larger and more important by the columns, arches and decorated mouldings which surrounded them.

The ground-plan of a Romanesque church is always in the shape of a Latin cross. The altar is at the east end of the **chancel**, in the direction of Jerusalem. The main entrance to the church is from the west.

In the interior a **screen** or **parapet** across the nave separated the congregation from the clergy and choir. In the eleventh and twelfth centuries there were no pews or chairs and the bulk of the congregation had to stand throughout the service. A stone ledge running round the perimeter allowed the lame, the weak and the old to rest during their devotions.

The **crypt,** which was on the lower floor and usually underneath the altar, housed the relics of saints. Because of its sheltered position the crypt is often the best preserved part of the church.

Window with decorated
mouldings

Arcades divide the nave from the aisles. Above
the aisles is the **gallery** (triforium), which gives a
view of the nave and was used by some of the
clergy during the services. Above the galleries
runs a narrow passage **(clerestory)**, in which
the principal windows are set.

This so-called 'three-tier' arrangement
varies from region to region. Indeed in some

Window with columns

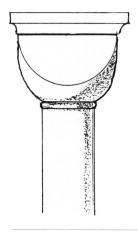

churches there is no third tier. In others, instead of a real gallery above the aisles, there is only a blind arcade on a solid wall.

The ceilings are colossal vaulted structures made of stone. There were two types of vault used in Romanesque churches: **barrel vaults,** which were the simplest kind, the shape resembling the top of a covered wagon; and **groin vaults,** those formed by two barrel vaults crossing one another at right angles. The seams along which the two barrel vaults are joined are called the groins.

Shafts rising from ground level up to the roof and transverse arches across the nave or choir give additional support to the roof.

Stone vaulting and stone walls helped to give a sonorous quality to human voices. The Gregorian chant developed during the Romanesque period.

Columns and piers are usually massive. The capitals are based on either the Roman Corinthian or the later **'cushion'** design. The latter has the shape of a cube, except that its bottom edges are rounded. The base of the column is made up of concentric circular

Three-tier arrangement –
exterior (left), interior (right)

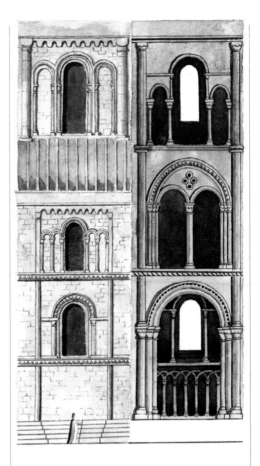

mouldings, the lower ones being wider than
the upper ones. The space between the
rounded base and the pedestal is sometimes
filled out with carvings.

Capital with carved figures

PILGRIM CHURCHES

During much of the period when Romanesque architecture flourished the practice of going on pilgrimages was widespread. Most pilgrims were drawn to Jerusalem, Rome or Santiago de Compostela in Spain. Half a million pilgrims were estimated to have passed through France in a single year.

The arrival of a large group of pilgrims affected medieval communities much as an influx of tourists affects modern townships. Among the provisions made was the building of hospices and special churches along the pilgrim route. These so-called 'pilgrim churches' were exceptionally large and are among the finest examples of Romanesque architecture.

Pilgrim church (ground-plan)

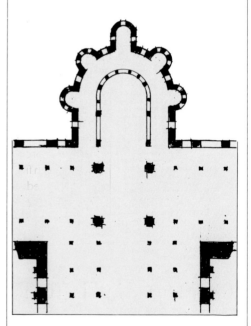

One of their features is the walkway behind the altar known as the **ambulatory.** This enabled groups of pilgrims to walk up one aisle, past the east end of the church, and down the other aisle without disturbing those at worship in the main body of the church. Small chapels led off

Side-chapels in a Romanesque church

the ambulatory, where the overflow of pilgrims could worship.

Because of the shape and size of the windows there is much less light in Romanesque churches than in churches of later styles. As a result the churches seem to us dark and mysterious. They did not seem so to the people who first worshipped there.

To understand how the church once looked you have to imagine it lit by many hundreds of candles and torches, the ceilings and walls enlivened with frescoes, and with many carvings painted in bright colours. Sadly, with very few exceptions, all the bright colours and the frescoes have by now disappeared.

ROMANESQUE SCULPTURE

At a time when very few people, apart from the clergy, could read or write the accepted ways of teaching the message of the Bible were by preaching, and by the carvings and paintings in the churches.

Carvings in a Romanesque tympanum

I am a woman, poor and old.
Quite ignorant, I cannot read.
They showed me by my village
    church
A painted Paradise with harps
And Hell where the damned souls
    are boiled,
One gives me joy, the other
    frightens me.

François Villon (c. 1431–63)

Many of the carvings tell stories, some taken from everyday life, but the majority from the Bible. In some churches a story continued from one capital to the next, and the worshipper might walk the length of the nave before coming to the story's end.

Medieval people were more accustomed, and hence better able, to follow the stories told in the carvings, but with a little patience and some knowledge of the Bible these stories can still be understood without much difficulty.

In Romanesque art sculpture was subordinate to architecture. In other words the carvings had to fit exactly into clearly defined spaces

Animal figures incorporated into a design

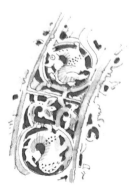

The flow of the garment created movement

such as the tympanum, capitals, arches or columns.

To fit the sculptures into their allotted spaces, the human and animal figures often had to be distorted. Bodies are elongated or bent, and heads and limbs are often out of proportion to the rest of the body. Surprisingly perhaps, these distortions do not detract from the realism of the figures. They even seem to enhance the power of the expressions in the carvings.

The elongated figure fits perfectly into the space allotted to it within a column. Movement and light are created in spite of the restricted space. The material of the garment is drawn tightly across, outlining the body beneath. Even the hem of the dress flares out as if caught by the breeze. It looks almost as if the material were damp and that is why it is clinging to the body. This style of carving is called '**wet draping**' and is very common in Romanesque art.

AROUND EUROPE

The Tower of Pisa

Italy

Both exterior and interior walls are frequently covered in marble. Rows upon rows of wall arcades, even extending on to the gables, decorate the façades of many of the churches.

Crouching lions and other beasts support some of the columns, symbolizing the victory of good over evil.

The southern part of the Italian mainland and Sicily were occupied at various times by Byzantines, by Arabs and by Normans. Each of these left an imprint on local architecture. Many of the churches are a mixture of Italian and foreign influences.

Germany

Some of the churches have an apse both at the east and the west end. In such cases the main entrance to the church is from the side.

Spain

From the 8th to the 15th century much of Spain was under Arab occupation and Moorish influence on Spanish architecture was widespread (see previous chapter).

England

In England the Romanesque is known as the Norman style. In outward appearance the buildings tend to be heavy, and they often have squat, square towers. In the interiors massive **compound piers** frequently alternate with equally massive columns.

In England the Romanesque is
known as Norman

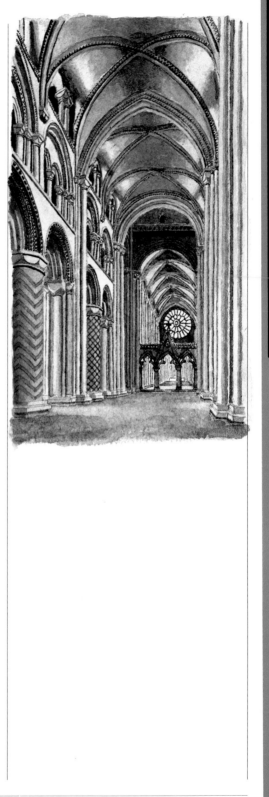

Chronology

1147	Second Crusade
1187	Saladin recaptures Jerusalem from the crusaders
1198	Order of Teutonic Knights founded
1209	Foundation of Cambridge University
1210	Mongols led by Genghis Khan invade China
1215	*Magna Carta* signed
1260	Kublai Khan makes Peking his capital
1275	Marco Polo reaches Peking
1306	Giotto completes series of frescoes in Padua
1307	Dante begins work on his *Divine Comedy*
1337	Beginning of Hundred Years' War between England and France
1348	Outbreak of Black Death in Europe
1358	Peasant rising in France known as the *Jacquerie*
1397	Union of Norway, Sweden and Denmark

THE GOTHIC STYLE

Figures from the exterior of a Gothic church

Mason's marks

Gothic architecture is the supreme expression in stone of the Christian faith.

Not surprisingly, the greatest Gothic buildings are the cathedrals, of which there was an astonishing outcrop in western Europe in the 13th and 14th centuries. Although Christ taught that the Kingdom of Heaven is within us, the spires and the internal structures of Gothic churches pointed upwards towards a heaven above.

Medieval communities took immense pride in their cathedrals. Some cities gave more than half their revenue year after year towards the cost of building them, but more was continually needed and city administrators often had to develop ingenious methods of fund-raising to meet these needs. The men who designed and built the cathedrals were not usually local people. They were professional masons, who were organized in lodges, and travelled from city to city as work became available.

The master masons were in effect the architects. A number of them are no longer known to us by name, although they are identifiable by the individual masons' marks which they cut into blocks of stone.

There were no architects' drawings in the modern sense of the term, and parts of buildings did occasionally fall down because of faulty construction. But the splendour of their achievements is the abiding proof of the masons' extraordinary skills and of the strength of the spirit which inspired them.

HOW TO RECOGNIZE A GOTHIC BUILDING

The **pointed arch** is the main feature which the visitor sees in a Gothic building.

CHURCHES

The western façade is the most ornate part of a Gothic church. There are usually three richly carved doorways in this façade, the centre one being the largest of the three. This arrangement of the doorways corresponds with the internal division of the building, which has a wide nave flanked by two aisles.

The deep doorways are formed by receding columns with arches above them. A characteristic feature is the so-called **column figure,** which is not in fact a part of the column

A richly carved doorway

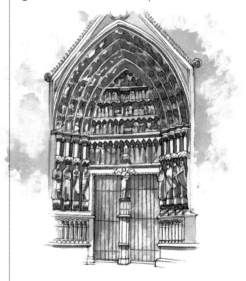

itself. In classical architecture figures are commonly incorporated in the columns, but in Gothic they usually stand in front of them.

The figures in Gothic sculpture look very natural. The drapery of the dresses is soft and pleasing. Many of the female figures have taken up a sinuous stance known as the **Gothic S-curve.**

Above the doorways the façade is so richly decorated that there are hardly any empty spaces left. Rows of sculptured figures alternate with niches holding even more figures. Many doors, windows and niches are surmounted by mock gables.

Horizontal mouldings and rows of blind

The material of this figure's cloak forms soft and natural patterns

A Gothic church

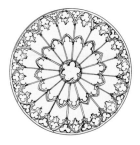

A rose window

arcades add to the richness of the fabric. A huge round window with intricate stone work, the so-called 'rose window', is usually in the middle of the façade.

Crockets are a typically Gothic decoration. They are carved in the form of curling leaves and are used to decorate the sloping sides of spires, canopies, pinnacles and other projections.

The carvings above the doors were intended to instruct. They were based on biblical events and, being in narrative form, often continued from one door to the next.

Above the western façade are the two main towers, and at the point where the nave crosses the transepts is the centre tower, which usually has a very high spire. The original intention in some of the larger churches was to build even more towers, but the plans were sometimes abandoned for lack of money or

Crockets

because adding further structures on top of already high buildings was thought too dangerous.

INTERIORS

The ground-plan in a Gothic church is in the form of a Latin cross. This was often modified by the addition of extra chapels or of double rows of aisles and ambulatories.

The nave is divided from the aisles by a row of columns. Above the aisles are the galleries, and above the galleries a row of windows. The arrangement differs from church to church, and to the visitor it can be particularly interesting to see the form these differences take.

Entering a Gothic church gives an immediate impression of vast height, which is created partly by the real height of the building and partly by an optical illusion produced by the columns, arches, ribs and other features all pointing upwards.

In earlier styles the weight – or the downward thrust – exerted by the heavy vaulted roofs was evenly distributed over the massive walls. Windows and doors were kept relatively small in order not to weaken the walls, and consequently churches tended to be dark.

In Gothic architecture the roof structure is of the **rib vault** kind. The ribs, made of stone, were constructed first, and then the space between the ribs was filled with a much lighter material. A further development enabled the bulk of the downward thrust to be carried by the ribs. From there it was channelled through the columns into the ground.

The function of the **flying buttresses** was to counterbalance any outward thrust exerted on the walls. **Pinnacles** on top of the buttresses look decorative, but their main purpose is to add further weight and stability to the buttresses themselves.

As the walls no longer had to bear so much of the weight, they could be built much higher

A Gothic church (ground-plan)

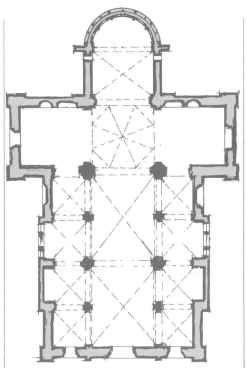

and with large windows, which allowed light to flood in to the building. Some of the windows were so big that they reached almost from one buttress to another.

A flying buttress

Daylight coming through these huge windows would have created a harsh and, perhaps in the minds of the builders, a too worldly effect. To produce a more pleasing and more suitable light the masons developed the stained glass window.

Walls could be built much higher and with large windows

A stained glass window

STAINED GLASS

Stained glass windows are among the great glories of Gothic churches. The art which produced them was similar in execution to that of the mosaic. A sketch was made first, probably depicting a biblical story or an incident in the life of a saint. A cartoon – or full-sized drawing based on the sketch – was then placed on a whitewashed table supported by trestles.

The next step was to mark on the cartoon the colours to be used. Glass was then cut with a fairly crude iron instrument to fit the shapes of the coloured sections as closely as possible. (When in the 16th century a diamond-cutting tool was invented which was also used for glass, all the greatest Gothic windows had been made.)

Details such as faces were painted on to the glass, which was fired in a kiln, cooled, and laid out on the table again. The gaps between the pieces of glass were filled with lead, which is both pliable and weather-resistant. One of the great artistic achievements of the Gothic window-makers was the way in which they used lead to create rhythm and to emphasize lines in their designs.

There were therefore four main elements in the art: glass, pigment, lead and, not least important, the light which filtered through the window.

When many of the windows were made there was less lead in them than there is today. As time went by, more lead had sometimes to be added and new glass cut as windows suffered damage from causes ranging from warfare to the flight of birds.

FURTHER GOTHIC FEATURES

Apart from the stained glass windows, the **vaults** are probably the most aesthetically pleasing feature of a Gothic church. As the style developed, more and more ribs, some purely decorative, were added to the vaults. The patterns they formed are often of extraordinary beauty.

Gothic columns are slim. Piers are often surrounded by a cluster of shafts and are known as **cluster-piers.**

Capitals are decorated mainly with foliage. In later Gothic both human and animal figures are found on the capitals. Occasionally one can come across the slightly disconcerting sight of a human face peeping out from among the foliage, with leaves growing out of his face. This is the Green Man, who in pagan times was a familiar fertility symbol.

A Gothic boss

Capital decorated with foliage

Foliage decoration

VARIATIONS IN GOTHIC ARCHITECTURE

The Gothic style in architecture lasted in some parts of Europe for over four hundred years. Its history can be divided into three periods: early Gothic, high Gothic and late Gothic. Each period had its own characteristic features, but probably the easiest way to identify a period is by the windows and, in particular, by the stonework within the windows.

Early Gothic so-called **lancet windows** are tall and narrow. When two or more windows were grouped together they were usually surrounded by an arch. The empty space between the top of the windows and the surrounding arch was probably thought too plain to be left unadorned. The stonemasons therefore pierced the stone and created circular, trefoil or quatrefoil designs called **plate tracery.** As the windows became larger they were given vertical and horizontal divisions, called **mullions** and **transoms.**

The high Gothic window is larger and the mullions and transoms are slimmer. The tracery here is curvilinear, sweeping in various directions. The pointed arch is often replaced by the **ogee arch.**

Lancet window

Circular tracery

Curvilinear tracery

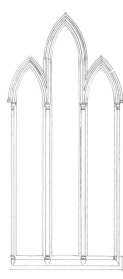

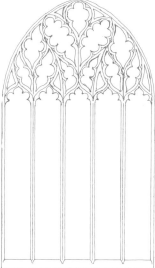

Window incororating an ogee arch

As a generalization it can be said that early Gothic and high Gothic are similar in style in most European countries. But by the time of late Gothic each country had developed a variation of the style with strong national characteristics of its own.

In northern Europe there was a tendency to build high, steep roofs and large windows letting in as much light as possible. In the south, where there was less rain and snow, the roofs were flatter, and to keep the heat of the sun out, the windows were smaller.

Smaller windows meant larger wall surfaces. As a result fresco painting continued in the south, and stained glass was much rarer than it was in the north.

England

In England the three main periods of Gothic architecture are called Early English, Decorated and Perpendicular. The first two were similar to early and high Gothic respectively. Perpendicular was a purely English style.

During the Perpendicular period in England the decorating of panels on both outer and inner walls was in fashion. The style was then adopted for windows, the glass being divided into small rectangular panels and the whole window being enclosed in a broad arch. During the same period vaults became more and more intricate, culminating in the exclusively English **fan-vault**.

One of the most pleasing aspects of an English Gothic cathedral is the amount of open space around it which enables the visitor to look at it from a distance. The reason for this is that in England the cathedrals were monastic establishments with considerable land of their own.

Apart from the churches a number of ornately carved timber buildings survive from this period, some of them private houses, some inns, and some town halls. Timber was also used for the roofs, outstanding among

English perpendicular window

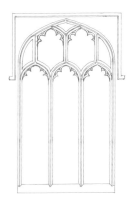

them being the beautifully carved hammer-beam roofs.

The final development of English Gothic is known as the Tudor style.

France

In France the late Gothic period is called Flamboyant, from the window tracery which resembles flames leaping upwards. Towards the end of the period the fortresses of the nobles became more like palaces. They still retained their moats and other defensive works, but the courtyards became more elaborate, and much more space was given over to living quarters.

The town houses of the rich also became more elegant and comfortable. Most of these houses had a spacious courtyard and were two or three storeys high. High roofs and **dormer windows** were characteristic features.

Germany

Among the peculiar characteristics of German Gothic architecture are the so-called 'hall churches'. In these, the roof of the nave and the roof of the aisles are of the same height. Some of the churches had only one central tower above the western façade.

Spain

In Spain the Gothic style is called 'Plateresque', meaning that it resembles ornate silver work. The decorations are exceptionally rich and cover most of the façade.

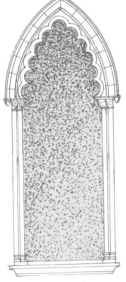

Spanish Gothic window

A Gothic cloister

Chronology

THE RENAISSANCE

15th – 16th Century

The term 'renaissance' – or rebirth – is commonly used to describe the great intellectual awakening which took place in Europe from the 14th to the 16th centuries.

In architecture the Renaissance style started in 15th-century Florence, and from there spread to most other parts of Europe. Just as the general intellectual awakening was stimulated by rediscovery of classical literature – the monk Rabelais declared that a man should be ashamed of knowing no Greek – so the new Italian architectural style was deeply influenced by the theory and practice of Imperial Rome.

In the early 15th century a ten-volume work was rediscovered in Italy. Its author, **Vitruvius**, was an architect and engineer who served the Emperor Augustus and dedicated his work to him. The book gave detailed information on the different styles practised by Roman architects and the rules governing correct proportions and other requirements.

Vitruvius was widely accepted as an authority on how buildings should be constructed, and some of the greatest Renaissance architects, men whose names are still household words, were close students of his work.

As the new vogue spread, architects came to Rome from other Italian cities, and then from other European countries, to study ancient Roman buildings – most of them in ruins. A number of them published their findings. New works were also produced known as sample books, which contained architectural drawings. With the advent of printing these were more and more widely distributed.

Renaissance architects did not try to make exact copies of ancient Roman buildings. In

A town palace

more than a thousand years the manner of life had changed too much for this to be feasible. But they did observe the rules and outward forms which Vitruvius had described in such detail, adapting them to the requirements of their own time and imposing on them, as great architects will, their own personalities.

Among the many features which they incorporated into their own buildings were the Roman arch, the vault, the gable and, most important, the five Roman orders: Tuscan, Doric, Ionic, Corinthian and Composite.

As a generalization, Renaissance architecture can be divided into two main periods: 15th-century early Renaissance and 16th-century high Renaissance. In early Renaissance, Roman influence is most apparent in the ornamentation of the buildings. In high Renaissance Roman influence extends to the structure of the buildings as much as to their ornamentation.

HOW TO RECOGNIZE A RENAISSANCE BUILDING

Renaissance buildings are chiefly characterized by their classical components and their very striking semi-elliptical domes. The greatest buildings of the period are town palaces, country villas, and churches.

TOWN PALACES

Medieval castles were fortresses in which large numbers of people could be assembled. Renaissance palaces, by contrast, were planned as agreeable places in which to live and to entertain. They often included store-rooms and offices, but they were not designed to be defended against battering-rams or bowmen. To prevent theft, or even an onslaught by an angry mob, the ground floor windows were always kept small and covered by a grille. The ironwork was usually based on Roman motifs. Above the ground floor the windows became very much larger and more ornate.

Roman influence is pervasive. The Roman amphitheatre may seem a surprising source of inspiration for the home of a Renaissance prince or merchant. Yet one look at an amphitheatre reveals how much the arches and pilasters on the façades of stately houses in Florence, for example, owe to the past.

Seen from the street, the ground floor façade is forbidding. It is often rusticated – that is to say the walls are formed of large blocks of stone with broad joints. In some palaces the whole of the façade is rusticated; in others rustication is restricted to the corner edges of the building.

Many of the early Renaissance windows consist of a single rusticated arch enclosing two openings separated by a single column. Later

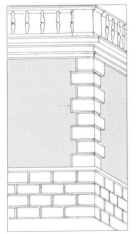
Rustication

83

windows are rectangular in shape, surrounded with mouldings, and with consoles and a pediment above.

Another type of window, which is also rectangular, is flanked by engaged columns – columns partly attached to the wall – which carry an entablature. The pediment above is curved. In a number of buildings windows with curved pediments alternate with windows having pointed pediments.

Doors are normally flanked by columns carrying an entablature. Pediments above the doors are common.

In the 16th century a Renaissance variation of the Roman orders appears. This is the giant or colossal order, which extends over more than one floor. Harmony and orderliness are still achieved, largely because the columns surrounding the windows are equal in height to a single floor and serve to indicate clearly the proportions of the building.

Cornices are a dominating feature of Renaissance buildings. Some jut out as much as

Window with a central column

Doorway with columns and entablature

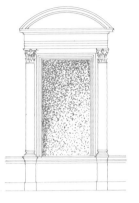

Window with engaged columns and curved pediment

2 metres (6 ft) from the wall. In some houses the top storey takes the form of an open arcade.

The ground-plan of a palace is usually square. The main entrance leads through the house into a courtyard where, as a rule, light and delicate arcades provide a startling contrast with the façade.

The façade is decorated with rows of pilasters placed between the windows. Following the Roman rules, the bottom row is Doric, the one above it is Ionic, and the top row is Corinthian. There may also be niches with statues and a fountain in the courtyard. Some palaces have more than one court. Staircases lead up from the courtyard, usually from beneath the arcades.

A Renaissance façade with pilasters, decorative staircases and statues

The mezzanine floor usually has square windows, and on the first floor above, the so-called *piano nobile*, the principal rooms are to be found.

In these rooms Roman influence is again apparent. The ceilings are either vaulted or flat and are decorated with paintings or panel work. The subjects may be historical or allegorical. There are few corridors, for the rooms are inter-connecting and decrease gradually in size from the main *salone* to the small *camera*.

Smaller palaces – or town houses – which had no more than two or three rooms on a floor were built in the same style.

Courtyard with arcades and pilasters

COUNTRY HOUSES AND GARDENS

The change from medieval fortress to Renaissance home was just as evident in country villas as it was in town palaces.

Medieval gardens, many of which were part of monastic establishments, were largely utilitarian. In 15th-century Italy, by contrast, the design of gardens for aesthetic pleasure and the integrated planning of garden and house was developed as an art form. Some of the greatest Italian architects engaged in garden design. This was in conformity with much of the spirit of the Renaissance, when one individual could achieve greatness as painter, architect, sculptor and inventor, and beings such as Leonardo da Vinci and Michelangelo were impossible to classify as practitioners of any particular art form.

In Renaissance gardens cypresses, plane trees, box and shrubs were planted in relationship to fountains, stone stairways, cloisters and terraces with balustrades, while the medieval tradition of the small, enclosed, private garden was maintained. Symmetry and proportion, colour and scent, light and shade were equally ingredients of the planned garden.

CHURCHES

The ground-plans of Renaissance churches

Circular Renaissance buildings recalled circular Roman temples

Both the inner and outer domes rested on a circular drum with windows all around it

The inner and outer dome

vary considerably. Some are modelled on the Roman basilica, some are in the shape of the Latin cross, and some are centrally planned.

The basilica-type churches either have flat roofs, as in the Roman prototype, or barrel-vaulted ceilings with domes. In the churches planned in the form of a cross, apses are often added at the ends.

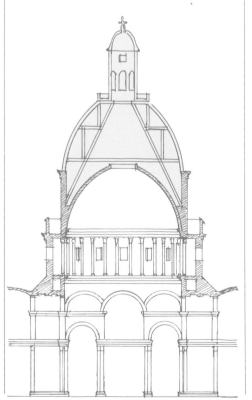

The inspiration for some of the circular churches came from Roman colonnaded circular temples. The similarity of the positioning of the columns is striking. The circular form was also held to symbolize the cosmos – conceived in the form of a globe – with man at its centre. Some of the domes were so large and impressive that they became famous landmarks.

Renaissance domes are spherical in shape and are constructed from stone. At the top of the dome there is an opening, called the **eye.** The dome is completely covered by a much larger, second dome. It is the outer dome, semi-elliptical in shape, topped with a lantern, constructed from wood and covered with lead or copper, which is visible from the outside.

Both the inner and the outer domes are resting on a circular drum which has windows all around it. Daylight enters the church through the windows of both the lantern and the drum.

Giant scrolls – a characteristic feature of Renaissance church architecture – fill in the space created by the differing heights of the nave and the aisles. Niches as tall as a whole floor with only one sculpted figure in them are also common.

Entrance to the churches is through richly decorated double doors. In some of the churches, there are a number of side chapels instead of aisles.

Medieval monastic churches had large rood screens which separated the choir from the rest of the congregation. These tended to disappear in the 15th century, the choir being removed to a chapel behind the high altar.

The ceilings in Renaissance churches are richly decorated, being either painted or coffered – that is, with carved decorated squares.

Among the features of these churches are splendid tombs, set in niches or free-standing. Some are truly magnificent examples of sculpture and stonework.

Renaissance sculpted decoration

RENAISSANCE DECORATION

A common form of Renaissance decoration is the **cartouche.** This is an ornamental panel in the form of a scroll or a sheet of paper, with curling ridges. It usually bears an inscription and is sometimes ornately framed.

Another characteristic decoration is the **sgraffito,** which originated in Venice. This was a manner of painting in which the undercoating was black. A thin surface of white was laid over it, and the design was then scraped down to the black background.

AROUND EUROPE

Renaissance architecture reached virtually all European countries and developed in most of them along similar lines. At first the Renaissance influence was to be seen largely in decoration. Gradually a greater understanding of the classical rules was achieved, and styles throughout Europe approximated more closely to those of the Italian Renaissance.

Spain

An ornate capital

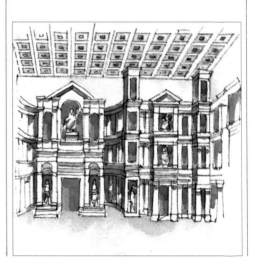

Renaissance 'Roman' theatre

Renaissance 'Greek' theatre

Renaissance theatre

Much of Spanish Renaissance architecture is known as 'Plateresque' – that is to say the surface of the building is almost entirely covered by carved or stuccoed ornaments. This practice was to be found too in earlier

styles, but there is a noticeable difference between the Gothic and Renaissance motifs.

Gradually a change took place from a quite stunningly over-decorated style to one which was much purer and in which some almost starkly classical buildings were created.

France

French Renaissance architects generally observed the classical traditions, but interpreted them in a style which is less severe and lighter than its Italian counterpart. A new order too was created, in which banded decorations served to conceal the joints.

In the 16th century a number of palaces were built along the Loire valley. Their situation was carefully chosen, most of them overlooking the river or a lake. Some were designed to ensure that maximum dramatic effect was achieved by their reflection in the water.

A unique feature of these châteaux is the grouped roof. Instead of one large roof there are a number of smaller roofs with extravagantly decorated dormer windows and chimneys.

Renaissance decoration

The Jacobean style

England

Renaissance architecture of the Italian kind reached England only in the 17th century. Before then strictly national styles prevailed

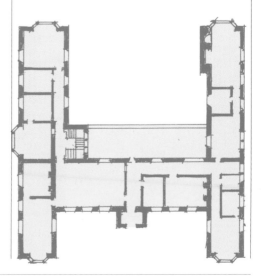

An Elizabethan house-plan

with Renaissance influence mainly in the decoration. These styles became known as Elizabethan and Jacobean.

Characteristic features are the E-shaped ground-plan, formal gardens, symmetrical façades, long galleries – intended originally for taking indoor exercise – and elaborately carved staircases. Classical details are to be found in the decoration. Oak-panelling and decorated plasterwork were used in the interior. Curved gables are another feature of the Elizabethan mansion.

The Low Countries

The outstanding features of Low Country architecture of this period are the high multi-storeyed gables. Medieval gables were stepped; Renaissance gables were curving, with scrolled sides and a pediment at the top. Many of the finials were carved in human or animal shape.

A multistory gable

Germany

Sixteenth-century German houses tended to be narrow and five or six storeys high. Gables were very ornate and curved at the side.

A Renaissance gable
(Germany)

MANNERISM

Renaissance architects
reworked classical forms

Mannerism is the term used to describe the work of certain Renaissance architects who used the classical forms, but in a manner which was different from the traditionally accepted.

Those whose work came within the definition of Mannerism included some of the greatest of all Renaissance architects, Michelangelo among them, but there were others who varied the rules largely through misinterpretation.

Only a limited number of architects or masons made the journey to Rome to study the original models. Many had to depend for guidance on the sample books, and hence their understanding of these classical forms was not always complete. In turn they had to instruct workmen, who might add their own individual interpretations. There was also a natural tendency for those who were accustomed to working in the Gothic style to continue to do so but to add Renaissance decoration.

The forms of Mannerism consequently varied considerably in different European countries, and it can even be said that in most of these countries early Renaissance architecture was a national form of Mannerism.

THE PALLADIAN STYLE

The term 'Palladian' is derived from the name of Andrea Palladio of Vicenza, one of the great architects of the high Renaissance in 16th-century Italy. Palladian buildings included churches, palaces, country houses and a few civic buildings (a theatre among them). Their influence was deep and prolonged, particularly in domestic architecture.

HOW TO RECOGNIZE A PALLADIAN BUILDING

The porticoes which decorate a number of Palladian buildings are the style's principal characteristic. Palladio developed this feature in the mistaken belief that such porticoes were to be found in Roman domestic architecture. No doubt his mistake arose from the fact that the Roman domestic buildings he was able to see were all ruins.

A Palladian *palazzo*

Palladian villa on a podium with symmetrical staircases and portico

Perfect symmetry is perhaps the second most characteristic feature of Palladian architecture. In some of the buildings the rhythm of void – solid – void is emphasized. The illustration (opposite) shows on the left-hand side the void behind the columns, followed by the solid building and followed by another void.

Palladian villas are built on podiums and were approached by impressive staircases. Most of the villas have rusticated ground floors.

A broken entablature and semi-circular arch

'Giant columns'

Two important features of Palladian architecture are the giant column, and the so-called 'Palladian motif'. Both were widely copied. The Palladian motif is made up of two giant columns supporting an entablature. Between the two giant columns there are two sets of smaller columns, each set supporting their own entablature. The two central columns support also a semi-circular arch.

Another characteristic feature, used mainly for civic buildings, is the broken entablature which juts out above each column.

VILLAS

The main building forms a perfect square. It is decorated with a portico on the outside. Some buildings extend sideways either in a straight line or in a curve. The extension usually housed the stables and the servants' quarters. Palladio himself likened his extensions to 'arms which would receive those who come near the house'. Some of the villas have porticoes on two or even four sides.

The interior of the house is planned around a central hall, which often has a dome above it. An elegant staircase leads up to the first floor, where all the main rooms are to be found. The rooms themselves are usually high and imposing, with large windows.

CHURCHES

A number of Palladian churches have porticoes reminiscent of classical temples. Giant orders give great dignity to the buildings.

Like a number of other Renaissance architects, Palladio experimented with the problem of how to balance the different heights of the nave and the aisles with that of the façade. He developed a type of façade which incorporated two inter-penetrating temple fronts which differed in scale. Perfect balance was achieved by having columns of different sizes. The columns backing against the nave are much taller than those which back against the aisles.

Palladian architecture had a considerable vogue in Europe, particularly in England, where in the 18th century there was an important Palladian revival. A number of the buildings of this period were almost exact copies of the buildings in Italy.

Chronology

1605	Publication of Cervantes' *Don Quixote*
1648	Peace of Westphalia ends the Thirty Years' War
1657	Dutch astronomer Huygens designs the first accurate clock regulated by a pendulum
1662	Royal Society founded in London under the name of the Society of Experimental Philosophy with Newton and Wren among its members
1664	British seize New Amsterdam from the Dutch, which they then rename 'New York'
1666	Academy of Sciences founded in Paris
1685	Revocation of the Edict of Nantes, which had granted freedom of worship, leads to a large exodus of French Protestants to northern countries
1687	Publication of Newton's *Mathematical Principles*
1703	Peter the Great begins building a new city which will be named St Petersburg and become the capital of Russia
1710	The first true porcelain made in Europe at the Meissen factory near Dresden
1713	Fahrenheit begins the use of mercury in thermometers
1729	Johann Sebastian Bach composes his *St Matthew Passion*
1742	Handel's *Messiah* first performed

THE BAROQUE PERIOD

Late 16th – mid 18th Century

The origin of the term 'baroque' is not known for certain, but it is believed to be derived from 'barrueco', the Spanish name for an irregularly shaped pearl.

Baroque architecture originated in the 16th century and was largely a consequence of important developments within the Catholic Church. In the mid-16th century an assembly of churchmen was held which lasted nearly 20 years. Its main purposes were to combat Protestantism, to pronounce on theological disputes, and to examine the need for reforms within the Church itself.

The assembly, known as the Council of Trent, created a new confidence among Catholics. Prominent among those who took part were members of the newly formed Society of Jesus, who emphasized the importance of an art form which could propagate the Church and all it represented.

In the churches, architecture and sculpture, painting and music were blended in a new and theatrical manner to emphasize Catholicism's vitality and to make its message attractive.

HOW TO RECOGNIZE A BAROQUE BUILDING

A sense of continuous movement, mainly created by the walls which alternate from convex to concave, is the most obvious feature of a Baroque building. Your first impression may well be that the building is in nearly every respect like a theatrical production. There is drama, there is movement, there are striking light effects and good acoustics. Wherever you are in the building you seem to have a ringside seat.

Baroque architecture, which originated in Rome, is a style for churches, palaces and

Convex/concave alternation and different sized columns on a Baroque façade

important civic buildings conceived and designed on a grand scale. In some respects Baroque is an extension of Renaissance architecture. Both have the dome, the column, the pilasters, the entablatures and other classical components. Where Baroque principally differs is in the freedom with which these features are incorporated, a freedom which no true Renaissance architect would have found acceptable.

CHURCHES

The undulating wall strikes one immediately as the outstanding feature of Baroque churches.

A Baroque church

Giant orders, usually two storeys high, and giant walls dominate the exteriors. Gables are broken or curve inwards before meeting at their apex.

Large windows are rectangular, and the smaller, more ornamental windows are circular, semi-circular or oval. Oval shapes are also used to frame wall carvings.

The ground-plan is often oval, which is the most fluid of geometrical forms and the one which most readily creates a sense of movement. The oval form is used throughout the building.

Undulating walls and rich decoration

As you enter the church the sense of theatre becomes even stronger. In many earlier churches there had been clear physical

Giant columns, ornamental
windows and statuary

divisions between clergy and laity. The
designers of Baroque churches wanted those
who came to worship to feel that they were
actively participating in the service. They
wanted them to see what was going on and to
hear the priest clearly as well as see him. Most
Baroque churches therefore have no columns
dividing the aisles from the nave; instead there
are side chapels lining the walls.

In the interior, as on the exterior, the
undulating walls give a feeling of movement.
The eye is drawn to the very elaborate
Baroque altar with a **baldachin** above it. The
baldachin is very much like a canopy, often
dome-shaped, and supported on four
elaborately carved columns.

Balconies, a natural feature of theatres, are
also found in Baroque churches, some with
elaborate ironwork.

Some of the churches are so richly

An ornamental window

decorated that it is possible to feel that the whole wealth of the Church is on display. This perhaps was the intention.

The combined efforts of architect, painters and sculptors produce in Baroque churches a remarkably homogeneous effect. Ceilings are decorated with paintings or with elaborate coffering. For wall decorations stucco was often used. Being a very pliable material, it helped to create the fluid lines characteristic of Baroque.

The rules of linear perspective, formulated in the Renaissance, were well-known to Baroque architects, and they used this knowledge to give an illusion of greater depth or length to parts of a church.

Column decorated with human figures

A Baroque palace

Light enters Baroque churches from very few sources, mainly from the central dome and any subsidiary domes. Light effects, particularly those achieved by the right quantity of light shining on to the right place, were an important, and essentially dramatic, part of Baroque church architecture.

PALACES

Many of the characteristic features of Baroque church architecture can be recognized too in the palaces. Among them are the undulating

Elaborately decorated
doorway

façades, the fluid lines both in construction and decoration, and the rich and ornate nature of the whole.

Monumental staircases are an important feature of Baroque palaces and villas. These staircases, some winding, others turning,

A dramatic Baroque staircase

A Baroque fountain (detail)

dominate both the approach from the outside and the interior of the house.

In country houses, and in town houses with space around them, the formal gardens were an integral part of the whole design. Some of the fountains are magnificent. In earlier times, fountains, even the more elaborate ones, performed a practical function. By contrast, in the huge and often complex grouping of figures in some Baroque fountains the only purpose of the water seems to be to add to the fluidity of the composition.

AROUND EUROPE

Italian Baroque spread to nearly all European countries, but it took root most strongly in central and southern Europe. It may be thought to have had its fullest flowering in Germany and Austria.

Spain

Baroque made a strong appeal to Spanish architects. In its most extreme form it is called 'Churrigueresque'. In this there is so much decoration that the structure of the building is barely visible. Characteristic features are twisted columns,broken and arched pediments and entablatures and pilasters with more than one capital.

A Baroque church, Portugal

Portugal

The outstanding examples of Portuguese Baroque are the great pilgrimage churches, which are usually built on hill-tops. They are approached by stone staircases, which are decorated by finials and sculpted figures.

ROCOCO ARCHITECTURE

Rococo decoration

The term 'rococo' is in fact an amalgamation of two French words; 'rocaille', which was used to describe the grottoes and rocks in the gardens in Versailles, and 'coquille', meaning a shell.

Rococo is often regarded as the last phase of Baroque. Although there are obvious visual similarities between Baroque and Rococo, particularly in the use of curves and ovals, the inspiration of the two styles differed greatly. Baroque was profoundly influenced by Catholic doctrine and practice. The origins of Rococo, which dates from the early 18th century, were much more frivolous and worldly.

In France at the court of Louis XIV, Baroque was much in vogue. Under his successor there was a reaction against the monumental manner in which the style had been used for personal aggrandizement. The number of pure Rococo buildings in the rest of the country is very few. But buildings with quite plain exteriors and brilliant Rococo interiors are much more numerous.

In Austria and southern Germany, Rococo took more extreme forms than it did in France,

A Rococo arch with scrolls and floral wreaths

Rich ornamentation at Versailles

S- and C-curves in decoration

and the style is more widely spread. Orders tend to be omitted or to be of little importance.

The style made its greatest impact in the decorative arts. Among the most popular decorations are scrolls and arabesques, shells and wreaths of flowers, all of them curving and sensuous. The decorations are often asymmetrical and incorporate many S- and C-curves. Rococo motifs can be found around windows and door openings and, in the interiors, around mirrors and paintings, ceilings and wall-panellings.

Colours are light and cheerful. White is used extensively on walls and blends happily with pastel shades and light gilding.

At one stage in the 18th century there was a strong Chinese influence in some forms of Rococo.

Chronology

NEO CLASSICAL STYLE

18th Century

Neoclassical architecture in the second half of the 18th century was in part a reaction to the excesses of Baroque and Rococo. It was partly a consequence of new discoveries of Greek

A Neoclassical stairway

and Roman architecture, and also to some extent reflected a climate of opinion.

It is easy to exaggerate the influence of 18th-century philosophers. The age was not entirely one of enlightenment. Nevertheless the concept of man as a creature whose life could be governed by reason was closer to the mathematical precision of classical architects – and therefore to their Neoclassical successors – than it was to the spirit of Baroque.

In the 18th century travelling became fashionable among those who had plenty of time at their disposal and the means to support themselves while they made long journeys. Greece, which was a part of the Ottoman Empire and until then little visited by western Europeans, attracted both antiquarians and architects, a number of whom published accounts of what they had seen. Two young British architects in particular, James Stuart and Nicholas Revett, spent no less than three years in Greece making accurate drawings of the remains of buildings, which they later published.

New light too was thrown on architectural practices in ancient Rome when the German

Neoclassical triumphal arch

poet and classical scholar, Johann Winckelmann, described the extraordinary finds which had been made at Pompeii, near Naples.

As a result of all this, Neoclassical architects could conform much more closely to the classical originals than Renaissance architects had been able to. In particular, they could model their work on the original Greek styles rather than on Roman adaptations of them. Some 18th-century Neoclassicists did, however, continue to turn to Rome rather than Greece for inspiration, and feelings between Greek and Roman enthusiasts at times became so heated that their differences were known as the Battle of the Styles.

HOW TO RECOGNIZE A NEOCLASSICAL BUILDING

Museum modelled on classical styles

Neoclassical buildings are characterized by clean, elegant lines and uncluttered appearances, and also by free-standing columns and colonnades.

The prototype to which Neoclassical architects most commonly turned was the temple, which was considered to represent classical architecture in its purest form. In the temples the columns served their original purpose: they were free-standing and carried the weight of the building. It was only in later years that they were used mainly for decorative purposes.

In Neoclassical architecture orders are also used structurally rather than as a form of decoration. Columns, free-standing and supporting entablatures, are more common than pilasters or attached columns.

Roof-lines are generally flat and horizontal, the roof itself often being invisible from the

A Neoclassical interior

ground. There are no towers or domes.

Façades tend to be long and flat. In front of them might be what was in effect a screen consisting of a number of free-standing columns.

The maintenance of the classical proportions on the exterior of the building was of paramount importance. The interior had to be adapted by the placing of doors, windows and staircases in such a way that nothing detracted from the classical perfection of the exterior. In earlier styles doors and windows might be treated as sculptural elements in their own right. In Neoclassicism they would as often as not be hidden behind colonnades.

These requirements left the architect with the problem of how to adapt an ancient style to meet the requirements of his contemporary clients, a problem requiring some ingenuity to solve.

Decoration on the exterior of Neoclassical buildings is reduced to a minimum. The craftsmanship is usually of a very high order. Stone-cutting, plasterwork and woodwork are more severe than in earlier styles, but no less excellent in execution.

Cumberland Terrace, Regents Park, London

The buildings are often massive and may seem severe. Some of them, particularly in the country, gained immeasurably from their settings.

In France and Italy the tradition of formal gardens based on geometric patterns was maintained. But in England there was a new vogue for parks and gardens largely created by man but designed to emulate nature. To achieve the required effect lakes and lawns were brought into being, hills were levelled, and streams diverted. Within these settings classical temples and sculpture were placed.

Houses were no longer divided from gardens by formal terraces but were immediately surrounded by them. The total effect, achieved in fact by careful planning, was of total informality. The 'jardin anglais' soon became fashionable throughout Europe.

The Neoclassical style, which became fashionable in the second half of the 18th century, lasted through the 19th century and is still very much in evidence today. In its purest form, in the 18th century, the finest examples of the style were civic buildings and private houses.

GEORGIAN ARCHITECTURE

In Britain, and to some extent in Ireland too, the 18th century left two great architectural legacies: the country mansion and the **Georgian city.**

The best of the Georgian cities were carefully planned, the planners having devised an ingenious method of giving a considerable number of people the impression that they were living in large and elegant mansions. Terraces, crescents and squares were created as single architectural units, all the houses having identical or closely matching façades.

A Georgian window

Many of the terraced houses, which now give so much delight to the eye, were put up by speculative builders. One of the great advantages of the style was that it permitted the creation of houses which gave continuous aesthetic pleasure but which were not necessarily the work of great architects. As the supply of great architects is at all times limited, this advantage was not inconsiderable.

Chronology

1815	Congress of Vienna redraws frontiers of Europe at the end of the Napoleonic wars
1823	Beethoven completes his Ninth Symphony
1840	Samuel Morse devises his code for sending messages
1848	Gold Rush in California
1851	Great Exhibition in Crystal Palace in London
1861	Kingdom of Italy proclaimed
1869	Suez Canal opened
1876	Alexander Bell invents the telephone
1877	Edison invents the phonograph
1887	Gottlieb Daimler and Karl Benz complete the first motor cars
1889	Paris Exhibition for which the Eiffel tower was built
1897	Rudolf Diesel produces the heavy oil engine

THE NINETEENTH CENTURY

Walk through almost any European city and you will find evidence of the 19th century all around you.

Those people – and there are many of them – who consider Paris the most beautiful of European cities, must acknowledge how much it owes to imaginative and dictatorial 19th-century town planning. Much of this took place during the reign of the Emperor Napoleon III, when the worst slums of Paris were ruthlessly demolished and replaced by the great boulevards and grand contemporary buildings which we know so well today.

Similarly in Vienna, with the creation of the Ringstrasse in the 19th century, numerous buildings were destroyed and a new,

The Eiffel Tower, Paris

monumental grandeur was conferred on a large area of the city.

Comparable transformations took place in Madrid and many other European cities.

THE INDUSTRIAL REVOLUTION

European architecture in the 19th century was profoundly influenced by the industrial revolution. Tasks which had earlier been carried out slowly and painstakingly by hand could now be performed both more quickly and more cheaply by machinery. Large numbers of people moved from country to town in search of work in the new factories, and the towns, as they expanded, needed new houses both for the factory workers and for their employers.

Buildings of other kinds were also needed to meet new demands. Among them were town halls, museums, concert halls, libraries, hospitals, department stores, shopping arcades, schools, colleges and universities, banks, offices, warehouses and factories.

Railway travel, which affected social life in so many ways, also influenced architectural practice. The first passenger-carrying railway in the world was opened in the north of England in 1825, and somewhat later railways, often constructed by British engineers, spread to other European countries. This is why in France, although cars drive on the right-hand side, the trains run on the left. With the railways came a need for new kinds of buildings, such as railway stations, railway hotels, goods yards and bridges which could carry heavy loads.

HOW TO RECOGNIZE A 19TH-CENTURY BUILDING

There is no single style which is characteristic of

A Victorian Gothic façade

the 19th century. Nevertheless there are some guide-lines which can help one to recognize buildings of the period.

Architects drew their inspiration from and copied virtually every historical style known to them: Greek, Roman, Romanesque, Gothic, Italian Renaissance, Byzantine as well as Chinese, Indian, Moorish and Egyptian.

Consequently, buildings are often more easily recognized as belonging to the 19th century by the function they perform than by the style in which they were built. For example, railway stations and railway hotels, department stores and office blocks are most unlikely to have been built earlier.

Some buildings were designed in a single historical style, with the fundamental rules of that style strictly observed. Others incorporated a blend of different styles used freely by the architect and with a disregard for the established conventions. A mixture of various historical styles within the same building may indeed be considered one of the

Brighton Pavilion, inspired by
Eastern styles of architecture

characteristic features of 19th-century
architecture.

Some styles were considered especially well
suited to particular buildings. Most new
churches were built in a version of the Neo-
Gothic, all other styles being deemed to have
pagan roots. Civic buildings were built mainly in
the Neoclassical style.

Another recognizable feature is mass-
produced decorative detail. Earlier hand-made
carvings were never quite identical. By
contrast, some 19th-century buildings have
considerable lengths of ornamentation all
exactly the same because all came from the
same mould.

DOMESTIC ARCHITECTURE

There was a huge increase in the population of western Europe in the 19th century. New houses were continually being built, both the mean back-to-back dwellings of the industrial towns, and prestigious homes for the newly enriched.

The well-to-do could plan their houses in the knowledge that plenty of domestic servants were available. The houses were spacious, and what today might seem a great inconvenience could be overlooked. Bathrooms with a direct hot and cold water supply were still a rarity, and hot water normally had to be carried. Food was sent upstairs from the kitchens.

Most houses, especially the grander ones, followed the general trend in architecture. Stained glass windows, patterned brickwork and ceramic tiling were all popular. The exteriors of many houses were notable for their wrought iron balconies and the contrasting colours of bricks.

STEEL, IRON AND GLASS

Iron had long been in use as a building material, but only from the end of the 18th century was it available in large quantities and comparatively cheap. Further developments in the technology of cast iron and steel followed which enabled architects to build on a new and massive scale.

There were also advances in the technology of sheet-glass making. The larger the sheets of glass that could be produced, the larger the windows that could be made. Earlier windows had comparatively small panes of glass set in a framework within a larger window. Now windows could be made from larger sheets

Newcastle Central Station – new developments in the technology of cast iron and steel enabled architects to build on a new and massive scale

A steel framework and glass façade

and the framework dispensed with. This was helpful both for domestic architecture and for the construction of shops, offices and commercial buildings.

The use of glass as a building material allowed architects to design conservatories on an

unprecedented scale. The techniques used in conservatories could also be applied to another 19th-century creation, the large-scale exhibition hall.

Joseph Paxton, architect of the Crystal Palace, which housed the Great Exhibition of 1851 in Hyde Park in London, began his working life as a gardener in the service of the duke of Devonshire in Chatsworth, where the largest conservatory in the world at that time was to be found. He later became a director of the Midland Railway, and it was at one of its board meetings that he sketched on blotting paper his design for the Crystal Palace based on the Chatsworth conservatory.

Possibly the most extraordinary feature of 19th-century architecture was that so many architects, while making full use of modern technology, continued to copy historical styles. A railway station might have a breathtakingly modern span of steel frame and glass over the platforms, but the façade of the booking-hall would be designed to resemble a Gothic or Tudor building. A bridge with the latest hydraulic lifting gear would be clad with stone to appear as a sort of fairy-tale castle, and a water-pumping station disguised as a Moorish palace.

The former classical gateway at Euston Station, London

This blend of the quasi-historical and the new scientific is unmistakably characteristic of the period.

Although much design was imitative and no single characteristic style was developed, great architects did emerge who stamped their personalities on particular buildings. This can be seen clearly, for example, in some Gothic-inspired late 19th-century church architecture in northern Spain.

The surrealist Gothic
Sagrada Familia, Barcelona
(Antoni Gaudi)

ARTS AND CRAFTS

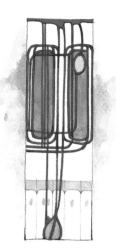

Metalwork decoration, Glasgow (Charles Rennie Mackintosh)

In 19th-century Britain a closely knit group of designers and writers staged a form of rebellion against the machine, which they perceived as dehumanizing life and producing ugly objects in large quantities. To express their beliefs they tried to revive ancient crafts and themselves created furniture and other objects of everyday use which were well designed and hand-made with loving care.

The name given to their movement was 'Arts and Crafts'. In architecture it was associated with simple, brick-built houses which at first were occupied largely by the middle-class intelligentsia. Features of these houses were gables, large wooden balconies and terracotta panels incorporating floral designs. The houses, some of which were set in carefully planned suburbs, all had sizeable gardens. The architects of the movement also designed some churches, in which the fittings were made by dedicated craftsmen.

Chronology

1903	First flight in an aircraft made by the Wright brothers
1909	Diaghilev launches *Ballets Russes* in Paris
1914	Assassination of Archduke Francis Ferdinand in Sarajevo leads to outbreak of World War I
1914	Henry Ford begins mass production by conveyor belt of Model T car
1917	Bolshevik regime established in Russia after November revolution
1921	Discovery of insulin
1926	Television successfully demonstrated in London
1929	Discovery of penicillin
1933	Hitler becomes German Chancellor
1935	Watson-Watt develops radio-location equipment, the basis of radar
1939	German forces invade Poland and bring about World War II
1940	Discovery of caves in Lascaux in France
1942	Construction of first atomic reactor
1945	First electronic digital computer built at the University of Pennsylvania
1963	Construction of Berlin Wall
1969	Armstrong and Aldrin become the first men to land on the moon.

THE TWENTIETH CENTURY

One of the chief difficulties in the way of appreciating classical Greek architecture is that there are so few buildings by which we can judge it. By contrast, one reason why modern architecture is difficult to appreciate is that there are so many. Nevertheless, there is clear evidence that many buildings of true quality and aesthetic appeal have been created and new and exciting styles of architecture established.

In many of the best 20th-century buildings the attraction lies in the lines and the shapes and not, as in many earlier architectural styles, in the decorations. Decoration has indeed been avoided, and this is another reason why the best modern architecture may not be immediately as appealing as, say, the best Baroque. Many people find that the eye has to be trained to appreciate the outstanding qualities of modern architecture, but when this has been achieved, the rewards are considerable.

Modern architecture, as the term is generally understood, began to make an impact in the years between the two world wars. There was no single style, and some of the greatest architects cannot be neatly classified as belonging to a particular movement or group. Nevertheless there were movements to which names have been attached either by the participants or by their critics. The following may be thought to be the principal ones.

ART NOUVEAU

Art Nouveau was the name of a shop in Paris which was opened in 1895 and specialized in the sale of household objects of new, as opposed to conventional, design.

The principal materials used by Art Nouveau architects were iron and glass, whose application was at first ornamental and later structural. Decorative features were curved lines and floral and geometric patterns. Examples are to be found in the flowing lines of prefabricated ironwork in the Paris metro. Others are in the Vienna underground.

Although some fine buildings were produced in Art Nouveau style, the movement was rather more effective in the field of decorative design. It was comparatively short-lived and came to an end with the outbreak of World War I in 1914.

ART DECO

Art Deco decoration, Milan Central Station

The term 'Art Deco' is derived from an exhibition of decorative arts which was staged in Paris in 1925. The association between Art Deco and jazz is a close one and the style has sometimes been called *Jazz Moderne*.

It is to be seen in many buildings constructed between the two world wars, the great majority of them serving commercial purposes. The style was thought particularly suitable for hotels, cinemas and fashion shops. Discipline is not very strong, and designers felt encouraged to let their imagination roam freely.

In essence Art Deco was a simplified form of classical architecture, in which the Greek and Roman orders were reduced to their simplest and then blended with motifs from other cultures. Such exotic intrusions tended to follow the fashions of the day: when Howard Carter discovered the tomb of the 14th century BC Pharoah Tutankhamun in 1922, the press treated it as sensational news, and for a time there were elements strongly suggestive of Egyptian art in Art Deco designs.

The materials used in Art Deco were

predominantly modern, chromium plate being particularly popular. More traditional materials, such as stained glass, coloured tiles and smooth render over brick, were also used, often in startling, jazzy patterns.

EXPRESSIONISM

Expressionism was an architectural movement which had a brief vogue in Germany and the Netherlands shortly after World War I. It was virtually confined to these two countries and was short-lived; by 1925 it had effectively come to an end.

There is a quality of fantasy in Expressionist buildings. They have outlines suggesting movement : swooping, curving roofs, spiky towers and much decorative brickwork. The shapes were made possible by the plastic quality of concrete, and the freedom of expression is sometimes more suggestive of sculpture than of architecture.

The Expressionist Einstein Observatory Tower, Neubabelsberg (Erich Mendelsohn)

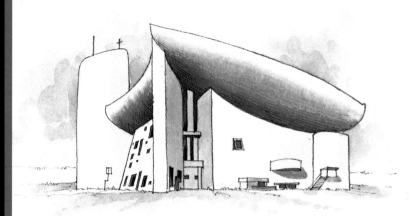

A 'Brutalist' church
(le Corbusier)

BRUTALISM

The term 'Brutalism' is rather misleading. It is in fact derived from the French term *'béton brut'*, which means rough concrete – in other words, concrete that is left unfinished, with the marks of the wooden moulding-boards visible on the surface. Normally concrete is surfaced with another material, such as brick, stone or smooth cement render, but the Brutalists thought that, in the interests of honesty or authenticity, it should be exposed.

There is also some connection between the Brutalist movement in architecture and the French movement *'L'art brut'*, whose followers specialized in rough-surfaced paintings.

Some buildings which do not show rough, exposed concrete have also been classified as Brutalist. In these, an exposed steel frame is visible on the exterior. Buildings of this kind are limited in number for in some countries – in Britain for example – the display of naked steel frames is discouraged by building regulations.

BAUHAUS AND FUNCTIONALISM

In the 1920s the **Bauhaus** art and craft school in Germany became perhaps the most important centre for the avant-garde in architecture – its director was always an architect – as well as for painting and the applied arts in Europe. Walter Gropius, the school's first director from 1919 to 1928, had been directly responsible for the construction of some steel and glass buildings before World War I which were of an entirely novel kind.

Teaching at the school was arranged so that pupils had to engage in a variety of theoretical and practical studies lasting for several years before they were allowed to design a real building.

Largely under the influence of so-called 'Constructivists' from the Netherlands and Hungary, teaching at the Bauhaus became severely functional. The doctrine was expounded that it is function which dictates form.

Under the Nazi regime the Bauhaus was closed, and a number of its teachers and pupils

A steel and glass Bauhaus exterior

The use of reinforced concrete, steel and glass removed many restraints in the design of buildings

fled to Britain and the United States. As a result, the number of pre-World War II buildings in Europe which can be directly attributed to the Bauhaus is limited. In the United States, Bauhaus influence was considerable in both domestic and commercial architecture.

The legacy of the functional approach to architecture can be seen in the new technology using building materials such as steel, reinforced concrete and glass in large sheets.

The adoption too of flat instead of pitched roofs has removed many restraints in the design of buildings.

HOW TO RECOGNIZE A FUNCTIONALIST

Because Functionalists were much more concerned with designing buildings to serve the purpose of whatever went on inside them than with their exterior appearance, surfaces tend to be impersonal. Sometimes, however, the shuttering marks on concrete were exposed in order to give an interesting texture to the external surface. The buildings are frequently asymmetrical, and the purpose they serve is often easy to deduce.

CONSTRUCTIVISM

Constructivism was a movement which began in the Soviet Union about the time of the Bolshevik revolution and spread mainly to Poland and Czechoslovakia, Germany and the Netherlands. In the Soviet Union itself few Constructivist buildings came into being, largely because of a shortage of the appropriate building materials.

The movement was the natural successor to Functionalism, to which it was closely allied. The Constructivists emphasized, and took advantage of, the possibilities presented by new materials. Steel frames were seen supporting the large areas of plate glass which were being made for the first time. The joints between various parts of a building were exposed rather than concealed.

In furtherance of the cult of the sun and of the body which was so popular in the years immediately following World War I many buildings had balconies and sun-decks. Windows too are large in order to let in as

Constructivists used large areas of glass to let in as much light as possible

much light as possible and are framed in metal. The exteriors are commonly white.

HI-TECH

High-Tech is the term applied to a style of architecture in which the services which a building provides and the function it fulfils are unashamedly revealed.

One way in which the architect achieves this is by ensuring that certain essential services, which are normally concealed within the building, are clearly visible from outside. Lifts travel up and down its front or sides. Escalators are suspended from the structure on to the exterior. Pipes for air-conditioning and water are not only visible but are designed as decorative features.

Bright colours predominate on the exterior. Pipework may be colour-coded to indicate its various functions. All the structural parts may be in one distinctive colour or clad in stainless steel.

One advantage of this style of architecture is that it facilitates the provision of large clear spaces within the building. For this reason it has been found suitable for offices, factories and even art galleries. The style has been defined simply as one which has 'the insides on the outside'.

A Hi-Tech building

POST-MODERNISM

Post-Modernism is a reaction or revolt rather than a single clearly definable architectural style. The reaction has been against the severity and monotony of much 20th-century architecture, and it has been felt and expressed by clients quite as often as by the architects themselves.

Post-modernist architects have continued to take advantage of the new materials available while turning to different periods of the past for artistic inspiration. There has for instance been a revival of the principles of classical architecture with emphasis on proportion and harmony.

Some architects have tried to achieve the

surface effects of Art Deco, though with the use of newer building materials. This has even led to the design of supermarkets in the style of palaces, and offices in that of temples. It is still perhaps too early to judge where Post-Modernism will lead and the potential value of its contribution.

BIBLIOGRAPHY

Brunskill, R.W. (1958) *Illustrated Handbook of Vernacular Art.* Faber Paperbacks.
Christe, Y. and **Velmans, Tania** (1982) *Art in the Christian World. 300-1500.* Faber and Faber.
Harris, J. and **Lever, J.** (1973) *Illustrated Glossary of Architecture.* Faber Paperbacks.
Jordan, R.F. (1969) *A Concise History of Western Architecture.* Thames and Hudson.
Pevsner, N. (1963) *An Outline of European Architecture,* Penguin Books.

Glossary

ABACUS	A slab of stone or marble placed on top of classical orders.
ABUTMENT	The wall taking the weight of an arch of a vault.
ACANTHUS	A stylized leaf used to decorate the capitals of the Corinthian and Composite orders.
AMBULATORY	A passage at the eastern end of a church which gives access to chapels behind the altar.
AMPHITHEATRE	A large open-air theatre with tiered seats.
APSE	The semi-circular area at the extreme end of a Roman basilica. This feature was later incorporated in Christian churches.
AQUEDUCT	A number of arches supporting, at the top, a channel along which water runs. First developed by the Romans.
ARCHITRAVE	The lowest part of the entablature.
ASHLAR	Smooth stone masonry in rectangular blocks.
ATRIUM	The entrance hall of a Roman house.
BALUSTRADE	The name given to a number of uprights, called balusters, which carry a staircase or support a coping above the cornice of a building.
BAPTISTERY	A building or part of a church in which Christians are baptized.
BASE	The lowest part of the classical column.
BASILICA	A Roman building used for administrative purposes. The early Christians adopted the basilica-type plan for their churches.
BOSS	The ornament at the intersection of the ribs in a vault.

BRACE	The diagonal, sometimes naturally curved timber between the horizontal beam and a main upright timber in wooden buildings.
BRACKET	A support projecting from the main wall, sometimes decorated with scrolls.
BROACH	An early English octagonal church spire on a square tower.
BUTTRESS	A wall built at right angles to the main wall. The projection decreases in stages towards the top in order to take the thrust of the arch or vault behind. In the later Gothic churches the walls were supported by arched, so-called 'flying buttresses'.
CAPITAL	The distinctive feature on top of the classical columns, whereby the different orders can easily be identified.
CENTERING	The temporary timber support needed in the construction of arches and vaults until the mortar joints set.
CHANCEL	An area in a church which is separated from the nave by a screen and in which the choir usually sits.
CHAPTER HOUSE	The assembly room for members of a monastery.
CLERESTORY	The wall over the aisles in Romanesque and Gothic churches which is fitted with windows through which light enters the interior.
COLUMN	A component of the classical orders consisting of a base, a shaft and a capital.
COMPOSITE ORDER	An order first used by the Romans. It incorporates the Corinthian acanthus and the Ionic volute.
CONCRETE	A mixture of cement with broken brick or stone, first used in buildings by the Romans.
CONSOLE	A projecting ornamental bracket.

COPING A covering of stone designed to protect the upper part of a wall from damage by rain.

CORBEL A projection of brick or stone used as a support. The word is derived from 'corbeau', the French for a raven, whose projecting beak a corbel suggests.

CORBEL TABLE A horizontal band of brick or stone carried by evenly spaced corbels.

CORINTHIAN ORDER A Greek order easily recognized by the stylized acanthus leaf on the capital.

CORNICE The top section of the entablature in the classical orders. Also the top, projecting feature of many external and internal walls.

CROCKET A Gothic decorative carving, often in the shape of a leaf, used on the slanted edge of a spire etc.

CRYPT A vaulted chamber under the ground floor of a church, often the burial place of a martyr.

DORIC ORDER An order perfected by the ancient Greeks and copied in later periods. In the Greek order the capital of the column projects from the top of the shaft in a graceful convex curve to the underside of the abacus.

DORMER WINDOW A window letting daylight into the space under a sloping roof. This space is frequently used as a bedroom. The word 'dormer' is derived from the French verb meaning 'to sleep'.

ENTABLATURE The area supported by the column in classical orders and consisting of architrave, frieze and cornice.

ENTASIS A device used by classical Greek architects to counteract the optical illusion which makes shafts with straight sides appear to curve inwards. The Greeks made the shafts curve outwards just enough to give the impression that the columns were perfectly straight.

FAN VAULT	A Gothic system of vaulting, in which the ribs start together at the main wall and rise in a curved fan-shape to a semi-circle at ceiling level.
FINIAL	An ornament which is the final feature of a structure, for example at the apex of a gable.
FRIEZE	The middle member of the classical entablature between architrave and cornice.
GABLE	The triangular top portion of an end wall where there is a sloping roof.
HAMMER-BEAM	A roof timber beam projecting from a main wall.
IMPOST	A projection, usually of moulded stone, from which an arch or a vault rises.
IONIC ORDER	An order developed by the Greeks, which has a capital, with four distinctive volutes on each column.
JAMBS	The sides of door openings. In Gothic main doorways they are often decorated with a cluster of partially rounded columns.
KEY STONE	The top stone in the centre of an arch. Until this is in position and set the arch is unsafe.
KING POST	A structure which rises from the tie-beam spanning the main walls to the apex of the roof.
LANTERN	A prominent external feature on the top of a dome. Often built in a classical style, it is a turret with a small round roof, which lets light and ventilation through the eye of the dome.
LINTEL	A flat concrete, stone or timber beam above an opening in a wall, which supports the structure above. In classical architecture it is known as an architrave.
LONG AND SHORT WORK	A form of construction used in many Anglo-Saxon buildings, enabling the corners to be strengthened by large stones. A flat corner stone was laid, on which a long upright stone was placed. This in turn was capped by the

next flat corner stone, and the process was repeated up to roof level.

MANSARD ROOF A kind of roof in which the lower, steeper part is nearly vertical and the upper part has a very low pitch. Named after the seventeenth-century French architect François Mansard, it was fashionable in Renaissance buildings in France.

MODULE The radius of the shaft just above the base in classical orders. This dictated the dimensions of all the other parts of the order and gave the correct proportions to the building.

MOULDING An ornamental strip in wood or stonework, either recessed or in relief.

NAVE The main central public space in a church.

ORDERS Upright stone columns carrying flat horizontal stone lintels, which are to be found in classical buildings. The proportions and interrelations of the parts were strictly in accordance with the rules for each order. Also a typical style of classical architecture.

ORIEL WINDOW A window projecting out from the main wall and carried on brick or stone corbels.

PARAPET The highest part of the wall above the beginning of the roof slope.

PEDIMENT The triangular part above the entablature in classical orders.

PENDENTIVE The triangular curved part of the structure supporting a circular dome over a square or polygonal area.

PERISTYLE A row of free-standing columns surrounding an area such as a temple; a court in a Roman house or a cloister.

PIANO NOBILE The floor on which the main room in a large house is situated. It is usually the one above the ground floor.

PIER	A large area of walling which takes the weight from an arch or a dome.
PILASTER	A square or rectangular pillar slightly projecting from a wall.
PLINTH	The projecting base of a building. Also a stone block serving as the base of a column.
QUEEN POSTS	Vertical posts used to support the main sloping timbers of a roof truss.
REINFORCED CONCRETE	Concrete in which steel rods have been placed.
RENDERING	The plastering of an outer wall.
ROOD SCREEN	A carved wooden divider between the nave and the choir in a church.
ROTUNDA	A circular building, usually with a dome over it.
RUSTICATION	Building stones tooled to give an exaggeratedly rough surface, usually with deep, recessed joints.
SHAFT	Part of a column between the capital and the base.
SPANDREL	The area above each side of an arch, bounded by a horizontal moulding above and a vertical moulding at the side.
STUCCO	A smooth sand and lime plaster, sometimes reinforced with hair, for covering exterior walls, often with imitation joints to give the impression of stonework.
TRANSEPT	Section of a cruciform church which intersects the nave.
TYMPANUM	The flat triangular space enclosed by the moulding of the pediment.
VAULT	An arched ceiling or roof of stone or brick.
VENETIAN WINDOW	A window with three openings, of which the central one is arched and wider than the others.
VOLUTE	The scroll-like decoration forming the main part of the Ionic capital and a minor part of the Corinthian and Composite capitals.

Building materials

STONE	Natural stone in its rough state is known as rubble. Stone which is decorative in appearance and has better weathering qualities is sometimes made available in smooth, rectangular blocks.
GRANITE	A very hard crystalline stone. It has good weathering qualities and is used on the exterior of buildings.
MARBLE	A comparatively rare and expensive limestone, which is hard enough to take a fine polish. Used for columns, pilasters and in thin layers for decorative purposes.
BRICK	A common building material manufactured from natural clay and silica, with a small amount of lime and oxide of iron. By burning in a kiln the iron is converted into red oxide. This produces red bricks. Blue bricks, in which there is a smaller proportion of oxide of iron, are waterproof and are used as a barrier against damp.
CAVITY WALLS	Two thin walls of brickwork with a space of about 5cm (2 inches) between them. Where external solid walls are thin, water is liable to seep through. The advantage of cavity walls is that rain may penetrate the outer wall, but the inner wall remains dry.
CEMENT	A building material manufactured by mixing lime and clay with water. The resulting slurry is dried off in a furnace, and the residue ground into a fine powder.
MORTAR	A substance used to hold brickwork together. It is made from sand and cement mixed with water.

CONCRETE

A widely used building material made of broken pieces of stone, brick or clean natural gravel mixed with sand and cement. Enough water is added for the cement to harden. Today large quantities of concrete are mixed in revolving drums and brought to building sites ready for pouring into position.

The Romans found a natural cement and used concrete for building throughout their empire. The knowledge of how to make concrete was lost after the fall of the empire and was rediscovered only during the Renaissance period. Even so, concrete was seldom used in buildings before the late 18th century.

During the 19th century concrete, largely because of its fireproof qualities, was used extensively, especially in commercial buildings.

REINFORCED CONCRETE

Concrete in which steel rods have been inserted. This enables it to support additional stress. In pre-stressed concrete steel wires are stretched by mechanical means and are then surrounded by concrete. The compression exerted by the steel causes the beam to be slightly arched. This enables it to take the load over longer spans, and less concrete and steel are required than in a comparable beam reinforced by steel rods.

METAL ALLOYS

Brass is made by mixing copper with zinc. *Bronze* is made by mixing copper and tin in various proportions. Bell-metal, for example, has four parts copper to one part tin. Silver is sometimes added to give a better ringing tone. *Iron.* Pure wrought iron contains no carbon. A small quantity of carbon (0.15 to 1.5 per cent) will convert iron into steel. A larger proportion of carbon produces cast iron.

Romanesque window with decorated mouldings.

Doric

Ionic

Corinthian

Composite

Gothic

Byzantine

Gothic

Cushion (Romanesque)

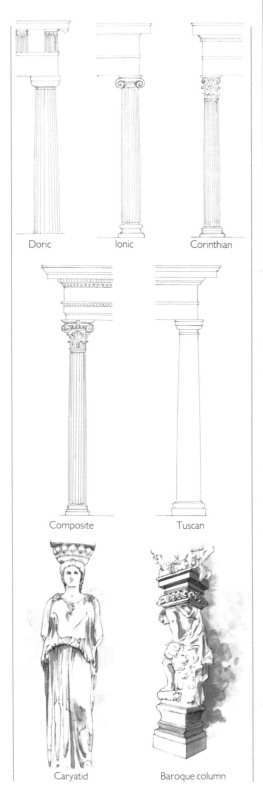

Doric   Ionic   Corinthian

Components of the Order
The column shaft rose from
the base and was topped by
the capital, upon which rested
at least three layers of
entablature: the architrave
(lower), frieze (middle) and
cornice (upper).

Composite   Tuscan

Caryatid   Baroque column

WINDOWS

Romanesque

Gothic rose window

Ogee window (Gothic)   Circular plate tracery (Gothic)

Renaissance   Renaissance

Baroque ornamental window

Georgian

ARCHES

Roman

Moorish

Romanesque

Gothic

Renaissance

Palladian

Baroque

Rococo

The Greek temple was often built on a raised podium. Columns (or orders), topped by capitals, supported the weight of the roof. Directly above the capitals, the entablature consisted of the architrave, the frieze and the

Doorway in a Roman house

Triumphal arch

Roman architecture combined the column with the rounded arch.

Aqueduct

cornice, upon which rested the roof. The entrance (or portico) was crowned by a triangular pediment, which sometimes contained carved figures.

Barrel vault

Cross vault

VAULTING

A Norman vaulted ceiling

Index

PHOTOGRAPHIC CREDITS

Front cover

1 *San Giovanni Fuorcivitas, Pistoia*
   Photo: Tim Scott

2 *Roch Castle, Wales*
   Robert Harding Picture Library

3 *'The Geode', Paris*
   Barnaby's Picture Library

4 *Nave, Rouen Cathedral*
   Photo: Marianne Majerus

5 *Glendalough, Ireland*
   Photo: Tim Scott

6 *Laxenburg, Austria*
   Robert Harding Picture Library

7 *Doorway (detail), Kings Lynn*
   Photo: Tim Scott

8 *Court of Lions, Alhambra, Granada*
   Barnaby's Picture Library

Back cover

Top *Osterley Park House, Middlesex*
Barnaby's Picture Library

Bottom *Wells Cathedral*
Photo: Marianne Majerus

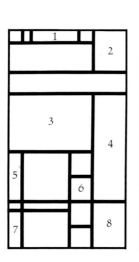